FACING THE OCEAN

One Woman's Courageous
Journey of Hope

Glena Davies

Published by
Hybrid Global Publishing
301 E 57th Street, 4th fl
New York, NY 10022

Copyright © 2018 by Glena Davies

All rights reserved. No part of this book may be reproduced or transmitted in any form or by in any means, electronic or mechanical, including photocopying, recording, or by any information storage and retrieval system, without the written permission of the Publisher, except where permitted by law.

Manufactured in the United States of America, or in the United Kingdom when distributed elsewhere.

Davies, Glena
    Facing the Ocean: One Woman's Courageous Journey of Hope
    LCCN: 2018952751
    ISBN:
        softcover: 978-1-948181-14-3
        hardcover: 978-1-948181-15-0
        eBook: 978-1-948181-22-8

Cover design: Joe Potter / joepotter.com
Copyediting: Claudia Volkman
Interior design: Claudia Volkman
Author photo: Terry Roueche

DEDICATION

This book is written for my son, beloved nephews, grandchildren, grandnephews, and grandnieces who have not had the chance to see the Africa that created the giants from whom they are descended. I want you to meet them here, so you will know and recognize them when they show up in your children and grandchildren.

It is also for all the sons and daughters I came to know during my medical practice years who gave me the chance to challenge them with my stories to persevere against the many odds they faced.

Finally, it is for you . . . anyone who would turn tail at the first sign of adversity . . .

"Dum Spiro Spero!"
While I Breathe, I Hope!

CONTENTS

Introduction   vii
One: Under the Cotton Tree   1
Two: 38 Upper Waterloo   11
Three: Pennies and Possibilities   25
Four: Dust on My Tongue   33
Five: Turning Points   41
Six: Tired of Chicken Wings   49
Seven: Tunnel Vision   59
Eight: Big Doors Swing on Small Hinges   67
Nine: Behind the Scenes   75
Ten: A Torn Letter   83
Eleven: Man of My Dreams?   89
Twelve: What More Could Go Wrong?   101
Thirteen: A Place Called Zorzor   111
Fourteen: Shifting Sands   135
Fifteen: The Match Game   155
Sixteen: Hershey—It Wasn't All Kisses   175
Seventeen: Living the Dream   195
Eighteen: Full Circle   201

INTRODUCTION

It was 1756.

Yeama, Saidu, Yeanoh, and most of their families had been kidnapped, shackled in chains, and taken to Bunce Island, off the coast of Sierra Leone.

They were about to be herded into a ship designed for two hundred passengers but had been refitted to hold six hundred slaves, stacked like cordwood with hardly enough air to breathe.

Just before boarding, Yeama looked east, facing an ocean of uncertainty.

Little did she know that they were headed to South Carolina to be sold to the owner of a rice plantation.

After the Revolutionary War in America, many slaves escaped to Nova Scotia as part of the black loyalist movement. In 1791 they boarded ships once more, this time facing west, headed across the Atlantic for West Africa and freedom.

The story you are about to read is about a young girl from Sierra Leone, who was raised with both hope and hopelessness, promise and poverty. She did not have a name like Yeama.

Her name is Glena Davies—a name familiar to the many descendants of slave owners now scattered worldwide.

Glena Davies faced oceans of her own, but one day she made a decision to sail her own ship and become master of her fate.

With a dream deep inside, she decided, "Do or die, sink or swim, I will give destiny a push, and nothing is going to stop me."

The purpose of this book is not only to chronicle the challenges faced by one woman, but to inspire young people that, regardless of their circumstances, with singleness of purpose, persistence, and God's help, just about anything is possible.

CHAPTER ONE

UNDER THE COTTON TREE

As a typical Class 4 student (the equivalent of fourth grade in the U.S.), I was always excited when our teacher announced, "Today we are going on a field trip."

My classmates were grinning from ear to ear. Instead of math or English drills, this was a welcome break.

I quickly raised my hand and asked, "Where are we going?"

"I'm taking you to the Cotton Tree," replied our homeroom teacher. She lived at Lumley Beach, just five miles from our school. She had lived on this estuary all her life, and her knowledge of its landmarks grew as she commuted back and forth to Freetown. At first, I was somewhat disappointed. After all, I had seen that tree at least a thousand times. How could anyone miss it? The giant tree, proudly reaching to the heavens, was the most famous landmark in Freetown, Sierra Leone, the city where I lived.

What I learned that day, however, did more than pique my curiosity. It was the key to unlocking a storehouse of information concerning my ancestors—and why I, as an African, had an Anglo-Saxon name like Glena Palmer-Davies instead of Bangura, Sesay, or Kamara.

Dressed in our school uniforms, we walked in single file down

Westmoreland Street, past the State House and Law Courts buildings, until we came to the roundabout where the famous majestic tree stood at least fifteen stories high—and the canopy of green covered nearly two square blocks.

Before we left, the principal had come out to admonish the teacher. "Be sure to tell them about the Nova Scotia Creoles and show them the Maroon church nearby."

My favorite math teacher was Heather Forsythe. She was no Creole, but rather a Canadian from Nova Scotia who had shown us maps and pictures of Nova Scotia. What was she talking about? I was mesmerized.

I had to pay attention as we circled around our teacher and she began to tell us the story.

"Do you see those huge buttress roots?" she asked. "They're big enough to shelter a six-foot man in a rainstorm—and that is where the first settlers found protection from the elements."

The Cotton Tree doesn't actually grow physical cotton bolls. It's in the Kapok species, and its cotton-like fibers are used for filling mattresses and pillows. What I really wanted to know, however, were details of the Nova Scotia Creoles, the Maroons, and all the first settlers. I had read about the slaves, their travels and hardships. But what happened to the children of the children of these slaves? That's what I was curious about.

A Brutal Business

Across the Atlantic ocean, toward the end of the eighteenth century, a war was raging.

From the time the first pilgrims disembarked from the Mayflower at Plymouth Rock in 1620 (in what is now Massachusetts) to the early 1770s, the population in the "Colonies" of America had grown to over 2 million—totally controlled by the British government. This included approximately a half million slaves, primarily from West Africa.

Captive laborers became big business for British ship owners, especially since slaves could be bought for twenty-five dollars in places such as Sierra Leone and Nigeria, and sold for over $150 in the new world. It was a brutal business. To keep men, women, and children from running away, ship captains would often cut off an arm or leg of a few slaves to instill fear in those who might entertain even the slightest thought of escaping.

The Revolutionary War in America was triggered when the freedom-loving Patriots claimed the taxes imposed by Britain were unjust. This escalated into boycotts, and on December 16, 1773, the destruction of a shipment of tea resulted in what is known as the Boston Tea Party. The British government immediately retaliated by closing the port of Boston and abolishing any form of self-government.

The fuse for a full-blown conflict between those loyal to the Crown and those who fought for a new nation was lit.

The Promise of Freedom

Thousands of plantation owners chose to side with the British. They promised their slaves, "We will give you your freedom if you will pledge your loyalty and fight on our side."

The offer sounded so attractive to the subjugated Africans that even thousands of Patriot-owned slaves ran away from their masters, gambling that England would win the war. Although blacks didn't fight on the front lines, they were organized into companies, including the Black Pioneers, who were scouts, trench diggers, and used for construction tasks. They wore blue coats with the motto "Liberty to Slavers" proudly embroidered on their uniforms.

History has recorded in gory detail the bloody battles of Lexington, Concord, Bunker Hill, Savannah, Charleston, and so many more. But the war was essentially over when a combined force of American Continental Army troops led by General George Washington defeated the British Army during the Battle of Yorktown (Virginia) in October 1781. Two years later the Treaty of Paris was signed, totally recognizing American independence.

Even before Yorktown, when it became clear that England would lose, the Crown issued a proclamation stating: "Any man who sets foot on British soil will become a free man." Perhaps the least-acknowledged, yet historically significant group of people, hold the distinction of being called the "Black Loyalists." These were the slaves who were loyal to Britain, promised a future of freedom, and left their mark on the world.

Starting on April 27, 1783, and for the next several months, boatloads of freed or runaway slaves left the docks of New York and sailed for Nova Scotia. The names and backgrounds of these three-thousand-plus souls were carefully recorded in two bound volumes prepared by the British with the title *The Book of Negroes*.

Such a document would not exist if it were not for the fact that the Confederate South wanted financial reparations from the Crown and the abolitionists. They had paid good money to acquire these slaves. This was their property, and if the British and abolitionists wanted to take the ex-slaves to Africa, that was their business, but compensation had to be paid.

The problem, though, was who was making the claims? And to

whom were the claims to be paid? The resultant *Book of Negroes* was based on information provided by the claimants seeking reparations.

Along with the promise of eventual resettlement in West Africa, the Black Loyalists were guaranteed plots of land in Nova Scotia. What they were given, however, was rocky soil located in remote areas. Most settled near the villages of Birchtown and Shelburne, becoming cheap labor for wealthy Nova Scotians.

Yes, they were finally free, but not much had changed. They experienced poverty, racism by the "white" loyalists, and endured the bitter winters of that frozen land. This led to the Shelburne Riots in July 1784.

The "Black Poor Society"

Meanwhile, in London, England, a crisis was developing.

Several hundred blacks, including many freed slaves from America, were impoverished and living on the streets in the areas of East End and Marylebone. To address their plight, a charitable organization called "The Committee for the Relief of the Black Poor" was founded. It became known as the "Black Poor Society."

On the test we took later that week after our field trip to the Cotton Tree, we had to name two members of the Black Poor Society. I remember writing down Granville Sharp and Lord Mansfield. A few years later, in another grade, the teacher read Lord Mansfield's speech at Westminister in London on the subject of slavery to our class. On June 22, 1772, he stated that slavery was "odious."

As part of the unit we were learning, our spelling word that week was *odious*—meaning "revolting" or "repulsive."

It was the use of this big word that helped pave the way to the ultimate resolution of the slavery problem. I made a note to learn and use big words. This became easier for me when Uncle Billy, a second cousin, gave me my first real piece of property: a brand-new dictionary, which I still own to this day. It became my constant companion. Every day I would open it, choose a word at random, learn what it meant on my way to whatever errand I had been sent, and then learn how to spell it on my way back. Over the years it has stood as a witness to the daily happenings of my life.

The Black Poor Society soon settled on a plan to offer the destitute blacks free passage to Sierra Leone. On their arrival they could set up a new community and enjoy the exact same rights as British citizens. Historians are divided on whether the motive was for humanitarian reasons (to get rid of a social problem) or the abolitionist's belief that they could halt the slave trade in Africa by spreading Christianity throughout the continent.

This was all done under the supervision of The Sierra Leone Company, which was not created as a commercial enterprise, but rather to establish a free colony in West Africa.

At the time, Sierra Leone was not an official nation; it was a land formerly called the Kingdom of Quoja. The new name was given in 1462 by Pedro da Cintra, a Portuguese explorer who sailed down the coast of West Africa. He called it *Sierra Lyoa*, meaning "Lion Mountains," for the majestic mountains that seemingly rose directly out of the ocean. It must have been during the rainy season, when thirty-one of the 120 inches of annual rainfall can occur in August alone. The rumbling thunder and dense vegetation covering the mountains looked and sounded like crouching lions to him.

Just over four hundred blacks survived the arduous 1787 journey from England. They built a small shantytown on the coast called Granville, named for one of the committee's leaders, Granville Sharp.

The Exodus

Meanwhile, Thomas Peters, a leader of the Black Loyalists in Nova Scotia, sailed for London to report on their grievances. On hearing of the new settlement in Sierra Leone, he returned to organize a mass exodus of disaffected blacks who were willing to begin a new life in Africa. They were cognizant of the peril their ancestors faced when crossing the Atlantic Ocean, heading westward and bound in chains.

This was welcome news, and over 1,100 former slaves—including entire church congregations—registered to board fifteen ships at Halifax, Nova Scotia, and make the crossing. They were intent on crossing this same ocean, but now facing east. The only chains they had were poverty and the fear of the unknown that awaited them.

It was a harrowing voyage, and sixty-four passengers died en route. The ships arrived at St. George Bay in Sierra Leone between February 26 and March 9, 1792. The town of Granville had been destroyed by invading tribesmen and a raging fire. The remaining original settlers were trying to rebuild at a new location.

The ships' captains ordered all the women and children to stay on board while the men disembarked to clear a roadway for the official landing. They hacked their way up a hill and through an overgrown forest until they reached a huge tree. With their flesh torn and bloodied from the overgrowth and their bodies physically exhausted, the men stopped and declared, "This is where we will build our new colony."

They had reached the Cotton Tree.

On March 11, 1792, they returned to the ships and brought the women and children to the site. Led by the preachers who were on the voyage, the people lifted their hands and their voices, singing:

Awake and sing
Of Moses and the Lamb.
Wake! Every heart and every tongue;
To praise the Savior's name. The day of Jubilee is come;
Return ye ransomed sinners home.

This was their first Thanksgiving service. The land was dedicated and christened "Freetown"—marking the birth of the political entity Sierra Leone (Sierra Lyoa). Small huts were erected before the onset of the rainy season, and the settlers and surveyors laid out Freetown on a British grid pattern, with parallel streets and narrow roads. A short while later, several hundred escaped slaves from Jamaica, called "Maroons," joined the "Nova Scotians."

The British influence in Sierra Leone is obvious to this day. The streets and neighborhoods I knew so well in my childhood were called Wellington, Bathurst, Regent, Leicester, York, Wilberforce, Signal Hill, Government Hill, Hastings, Waterloo, and Gloucester. Even the demarcation of the city of Freetown into East End and West End was copied exactly as it had been in the 1860s in Victorian London. The East End housed the poorest of the poor, while the well-to-do found themselves on the West End. If you examine the maps of British colonies established during this period in places such as Barbados, Jamaica, Bahamas, St. Martin, or St. Thomas, Virgin Islands, you will find many of the same names.

Written in the Book

After filling in many of the blanks on how the nation I called home came into existence, I was still curious about my Anglo Saxon family names—four in particular.

On my father's side, his dad's surname was Davies, and his mother was a Palmer. Thompson and Roberts came from my mother's lineage. Records show that slaves, property of their masters, were named in much the same way as an entrepreneur would name his product; Ford, J.C. Penny, and so on. These descendants arrived in Freetown owning only the names forced upon their forefathers a few generations back.

The Book of Negroes, containing the names of Black Loyalists who journeyed to New York and boarded vessels bound for Nova Scotia in the spring of 1783, became invaluable in my search. When I carefully examined those three thousand-plus entries, the evidence sprang to life.

- On the ship *Nisbett,* bound for Port Matton on the southeast coast of Nova Scotia: Phillip Thompson, age twenty-four, "formerly slave to James Thompson, Charlestown, South Carolina"
- On the vessel *Polly,* headed for Port Roseway: Ben Moses and Hannah Palmer—freed slaves from Frogs Neck, New York (at the time a British-controlled peninsula on Long Island Sound near present-day Bronx)
- On ship *L'Abondance,* also bound for Port Roseway: Jane Roberts, age twenty-three, "former slave from Charlestown, South Carolina"

The family name Davies was not traced through Nova Scotia, but it is believed that my father's ancestors were part of the Maroons, escaped slaves from Jamaica, since Davies is a documented name of numerous slave owners on that Caribbean island. Plus, many Maroons settled in the village of Waterloo, just a few miles south of Freetown. This is where my father, Joshua Okoro Palmer-Davies, and his father, Isaac Beresford Davies, and Mary Cordelia Palmer, his mother, were born. They are all buried in Waterloo.

These were the settlers who made their way to Sierra Leone, kept their names, thrived—and their children's children bore children.

To this day Sierra Leone Creoles visit and pay tribute to the Cotton Tree, offering thanks to their ancestors for the huge price that was paid for their freedom.

CHAPTER TWO

38 UPPER WATERLOO

How could a child who had been raised properly, attended private schools, and whose father was a high-ranking government employee be living a practically hand-to-mouth existence? How was it possible?

One day my grandmother told me, "Glena, when you are walking home from school, stop at Morgan Pharmacy and collect a few cardboard boxes." When I gave them to her, she had me put my feet down on the cardboard. She then traced them out, cut the pattern with scissors, and placed the inserts into my worn out shoes so I could wear them a few more days. This happened over and over again.

The country of my birth, Sierra Leone, gained its independence from Great Britain in 1961, ten years after I was born. Instead of an economy previously tied to the British pound, the currency was now going to be the "Leone." By the time I was a teenager, due to a series of military coups and political upheaval, the currency was in free-fall, and had been so devalued that trying to eke out a living was challenging, to say the least.

Life on the Compound

On a map of Sierra Leone, one can see an island just off the southwest coast of the country called Sherbro, and a town of about ten thousand residents called Bonthe. That's where I was born. The major industry is fishing, and it was the center of our family's life.

Since we had little access to milk, cheese, and other dairy products, we ate fish—boiled, fried, and cooked every way you can think of. When anyone went to the fish market, my grandmother would remind them, "Make sure it didn't die twice!" Most of the sellers had their catch tied to a post with string, and when they would pull it out of the water, the fish would be thrashing around, so you knew it was fresh.

I was the third of four children. The first to greet the world was Olive May, the second was Gloria Claudia, and later would come the desired son, Ian.

The only way I can describe the house we lived in at Bonthe is to call it a compound. The land had been in my grandmother's family for years. It was where she and her multiple siblings lived communally and raised their children after their parents died. The home was big enough to hold at least six adults, their offspring, and other children my grandmother cared for, who had been abandoned or otherwise placed in her care for reasons unknown to me.

I was about four years old when I moved with my parents to the big city of Freetown. Olive and Gloria remained in the Bonthe compound to continue their education until appropriate schooling could be arranged in Freetown.

I still remember the school building across from the house. I was not enrolled, so I didn't have a uniform to wear. My poor grandmother endured the daily commotion I created because I wanted so desperately to be a student. She would patiently stand and wait for me to complete my tantrum, and then we would walk past the big, flowering jasmine bush that decorated the front of the house. I remember the wafting aroma of the flowers as I brushed past it. My grandmother always pronounced it "jess-a-mine."

African Roots

When shiploads of slaves returned to West Africa, most landed in Freetown, but they didn't all put down roots there. Some spread around Freetown, but many journeyed down the coast to Liberia, Ghana, or Nigeria. It was not unusual for African parents to give their children at least one name tied to their ancestry. For example, my middle name is Ojumeri, and my brother Ian's middle name is Olufemi.

My father, Joshua Okoro Palmer-Davies, became a horticulturist. He was loyal to his African heritage. Even though he studied in the United States and England, he never entertained thoughts of emigrating. After receiving a master's degree in agriculture, he held a high-ranking position in the Sierra Leone government, first overseeing those working with farm machinery and later determining the price of cocoa, rice, pork bellies, etc., with the Ministry of Agriculture.

As a result of his work, my father spent weeks away from our home at 38 Upper Waterloo Street in Freetown, which was approximately half a mile from the Cotton Tree in the center of town. We were neither East Enders nor West Enders. He taught agriculture at Njala University, about 170 miles away. He also spent much of his time in what is called the "up country," conducting experiments with rice production, teaching grafting techniques, and more. He had a first-hand knowledge of every district of Sierra Leone.

During the rainy season, my mother—we called her "Sisi"—would pack us up and take us to stay with my father at one of the Senior Service Quarters the government provided. There we enjoyed the luxury of flush toilets. In my mind's eye I can see my dad hanging a ham to cure and slicing generous slabs of bacon for breakfast. We had come a long way; this was a pretty good lifestyle.

As a youngster I was a bit of a tomboy. My two sisters were very ladylike and somewhat introverted. I was the opposite; I was very outgoing, and my mom once commented that I was like a son. She would even make clothes out of tougher fabric for me because she knew how much I liked to roughhouse and climb trees.

Once, when I was seven, Dad told us about a communal rice harvest he needed to attend. I begged to go with him, but my mother wouldn't hear of it. However, I raised such a ruckus that my exasperated father took my hand, pulled me into the back seat of our car, and took off.

It was a tradition in this particular area that, at harvest time, all the villagers would support one farmer and help gather his crops. That farmer, in turn, would reciprocate the favor for the next neighbor.

The oldest females would remain back in the village with two or three breast-feeding women who nursed all the infants communally. The others in the village would then go "bolleh," meaning they would harvest the rice. The women who stayed back were responsible for preparing a hearty meal for everybody upon their return.

When we arrived on the scene, the women were chasing chickens in preparation for the meal. Dad went out into the fields with the chief and left me with the older women and a few young girls. When they roasted peanuts, I was delighted that they shared some with me. They picked coconuts, and the water inside them was very refreshing in the heat. The soup they made was loaded with chicken and tasted delicious. It was an all-day eating fest for me—and I loved it!

As we were about to leave, the chief handed my dad a rooster as a "thank-you" gift for supervising the harvest. Just as I tried to climb into the car, it started moving. My dad hollered out the window, "I just married you off to the chief, and this rooster is my prize!"

Of course, it was a joke, and he was laughing his head off! That lively rooster and I ended up being companions in the back seat all the way home. My dad had a quirky sense of humor, which always amused me.

The Decreasing Stipends

My father proudly drove a big, black, British-made Vanguard; the four-door sedan was very impressive to me. The number on the license plate was C48. That identification number became significant in an unexpected event that occurred later.

The government stipulated that men with children who were separated from their family because of duty would receive a stipend in addition to their salary. Whatever stipend he received, Dad only allowed my mom five Leones per child per month until that child graduated from school. This was during the time of the monetary transition from the British pound to the Leone. Both currencies were used in Sierra Leone for a while.

For several years, life was relatively good. We were well-fed, well-clothed, and well-educated. Then, financially, the bottom fell out—not just for our family, but for practically the entire nation. The currency had depreciated to the point that it seemed to be worth less than the paper on which it was printed. The allowance from Dad remained unadjusted.

When I was about eight or nine, my mom's mother, Constance, moved from Bonthe and came to live with us. She brought with her a boy named Henry who was three years younger than me. He was the son of her brother, Solomon. Since our house had limited space, he slept in the same bed as my grandmother. When he grew older, he slept on the floor beside her bed.

The monthly stipend my father sent didn't go far, and financially we continued to fall further and further behind.

Sisi made the food stretch as far as possible. Meals were dished out on enamel plates and each child fought over whichever color plate was their favorite. Grandma Constance always took her portion of the meal to her room, where she shared it with Henry. Somehow Henry never seemed to have his own plate.

The Goat

Another month . . . it seemed like the £20 only lasted twenty-eight days. By the twenty-ninth day there was no food, no soap, no way to clean the laundry. We could sweep, or sleep, or read, or find some other distraction.

My distraction was going to visit my friend Rachel. There was always something going on at her house. Even as I approached the gate, I could hear the bedlam. I started to smile—it was better than reading and sleeping, only to wake up, read some more, and fall asleep again in an attempt to keep the stomach-growling to a minimum.

I pushed the gate open, thankful for the anticipated distraction of acting silly with my friend. It was a good pastime.

There on the ground was a £20 note, folded and crisp. I looked at the unmistakable purple paper with the picture of Queen Elizabeth II. My heart was beating so loudly I could hear it! I picked it up, examined it carefully, then refolded it and put it in my bosom.

What perhaps was but a few moments seemed like hours. Pictures of beef stew, sardines, corned beef, bread with butter, and Ovaltine swam in my head. What *can't* £20 buy? More loud laugher broke my revelry. I turned to the noise and there was a tethered goat, with everyone circling around it, trying to feed it.

"What are you doing?" I asked.

"They say a goat will eat anything, so we are trying to feed it some paper," said Rachel's cousin.

"How about this tin can or walking stick?" asked one of Rachel's sisters, which brought more peals of laughter.

"How about your mom's mother's Union hat?" I added. Rachel and I were now doubled over in raucous laughter as we let our imaginations run wild.

"Perhaps the goat would eat Freddie's ears?" she added. (Freddie had small, pointy ears.)

No one was paying attention to anything but the goat until Mabel, another sister, shrieked, "Oh my God, Mama will be home soon, and I haven't even gone to market yet," as she grabbed the market bag and headed out the gate.

A few minutes later she returned, wailing. Her scream marked time with the thud as my heart sank to my feet. Swiftly fading into the distance were the butter, beef stew, sardines, and corned beef. I felt it before she said it: "I can't find the £20 Mama gave me this morning for the market."

I froze in place as my left breast began to itch. The laughter was gone. All of Rachel's siblings now skirted around to catch up on the chores they had neglected in pursuit of finding things to feed the goat.

Mabel was distraught, pacing and screaming, while the thud of my heart slowly marked time with my stomach growls. The image was now a mixture of more wailing as I pictured their mother yelling and scolding them for not doing their chores—Mabel getting the brunt of the punishment. The next scene was of all us marching to the churnings of our empty stomachs the next day since they, too, would now have no food.

The itching grew worse.

The siblings started to argue between themselves. "I'm not going to go hungry because of your carelessness," said one.

"I had it in my hand," Mabel exclaimed.

"Then where did you put it?"

Back and forth they darted in search of the £20 note.

"Perhaps the goat ate it!" I shouted, now relieved that the itching was gone. Yes, that's it! My solution was perfect—the goat ate it! The punishment wouldn't be so bad now if the money had innocently slipped from Mabel's hand and the animal had eaten it. I could now definitely smell beef stew with Irish potatoes on the side.

Just this once perhaps Rachel's family could manage. We did it month after month, so maybe God knew I'd had enough. I was tired of looking for the telltale signs each day I came home from school whether I was going to eat or not. A cleanly swept yard? No smoke from the kitchen window made my heart sink. Wait! A bundle of unsplit wood in the yard . . . could it be? Wood means fire . . . fire means cooking . . . cooking what?

I would eagerly volunteer to split the wood, only to have Mama tell me it wasn't ours. So let it be *their* turn.

Words from Mama

I turned to go home. It was then I thought I heard Grandma Constance's voice (we called her "Mama") saying, "What you do or do *not* do affects others, and you too."

I remember her telling me that as young girl she lived happily on

Bonthe Island with her loving parents and siblings. They could walk to the beach to catch crabs, clams, dig up cassava, and pick bananas or plantains. So they didn't go hungry very often. Sometimes there would be so much bounty that the children wished they didn't have the visitors their parents would always invite to share their food; it would have meant more for them. Back then people walked for hours to visit relatives. There were no telephones.

Mama related the story that one day her mother had prepared a hen, along with freshly harvested plantains and "kiss me"—small, spiral-shaped crustaceans which, when boiled, could be brought to the lips and the meat and juice sucked out (hence the name "kiss me").

Her parents loved serving this to her and her siblings. They were easy for the children to eat, but they couldn't always have them as they were small and required a lot of effort to collect and make sand-free.

Mama's mom also had promised her that if there were eggs inside the hen, she would be sure to get some. Her mom was stirring the "Ebe" stew when word came from one of the boys who had gone to the village well to get water that a single file of relatives were heading for the house.

Mama said that her heart sank. It must have been the very sad look of disappointment on her face that made her mother agree to hide the pot under the bed and then send the older children scurrying to the wharf to get fish and dig up cassava as she quickly tried to put together a boiled fish stew. Satisfied with the dinner which they ate hungrily, the relatives were offered seconds. The children didn't mind. Their secret was safe.

After the guests left later that evening, her mother started the embers of coal to warm up the pot of Ebe that had gone cold under the bed. To her chagrin, the dog—who had stayed out of sight and was now sleeping contentedly by the fire—had devoured the entire pot of Ebe stew. That's when she looked deeply into my eyes and said, "Glena, what you do or do *not* do affects others, and you too."

Back at Rachel's house, my hand was on the gate, but my body did not move to exit. It was time for plan B.

"Hey everybody," I called out. "How about if we each spread out throughout the house to look more carefully? And Mabel, where were you standing when your mom gave you the money?"

Then I said, "Rachel, you go upstairs. Perhaps it fell when Mabel was going to get dressed."

And, "Tina, go to the kitchen where you went to look for those cans to feed the goat." Everyone dispersed.

I chose the area by the gate. Within minutes I yelled, "Hey everybody, come quick! I found it!"

I had pulled the £20 note from my bosom. The itching had stopped, and I was feeling very sleepy. It was time for me to go to bed.

"Mabel, it must have fallen by the gate."

"Yeah," she replied. "Mama was in a hurry this morning. I had to walk to the gate with her while she was telling me what to get from the market."

That teachable moment has lasted a lifetime. Personal adversity is no excuse from keeping moral obligations.

Keeping Up Appearances

As life went by, it seemed that my father would be gone from home for longer and longer periods of time. Financially everything seemed to be on a downward spiral. When my oldest sister, Olive, graduated from Freetown Secondary School for Girls, the stipend from my father was reduced to £15 a month. Gloria and I finished school together (I received a double-promotion one year), and the monthly cheque was now only £5. Something had to give!

Even though my mother suffered from problems with her eyesight, she began to bring in a little extra money making clothes with her prized Singer sewing machine. She was very talented in this area and could look at any stylish outfit and duplicate it almost exactly. However, my own clothes were hand-me-downs. When Olive outgrew them, they were passed down to Gloria, and finally to me.

The economy of Sierra Leone had become so out of control, despair was setting in. If my father was receiving an increased amount of money for the family, we certainly were unaware of it.

As if the end-of-month anxiety wasn't stressful enough, one month, instead of the envelope containing the stipend from our dad, we received a copy of an official-looking letter he had sent to the Ministry of Agriculture and the Ministry of Education. It read: "Failure to remit separation allowance funds will be detrimental to the children."

"What does detrimental mean?" asked Gloria, as she cowered in the corner. All eyes were now on me.

"Go get your dictionary," Mama said. After I read the list of synonyms out loud, Gloria wailed, "I knew this was bad," to which I replied, "It's not just bad, Glo—it is injurious!" And we both wailed even more.

My mother, a very proud woman, had to cut every corner possible just to survive. In her mind, being married to a prominent man in the Senior Service with the name Palmer-Davies meant that she had a reputation to uphold. There was no way she was going to step out of the house and look "woegry"—a word coined by my dad. He used it to express exaggerated consternation and disapproval of anyone dressing like Cinderella.

My brother inherited what I call the "dapper gene" twice over—one from his mother, who knew just how to be impeccably dressed, and the other from his father, with his anti-woegry viewpoint. I, on the other hand, have always chosen comfort over style. It was easy for me to slip into my sisters' old clothes; as long as it was comfortable, I cared nothing about style. This may explain why, when someone asks me, "Is that what you are wearing?" I feel like answering, "No, just while you are nagging me!"

It wasn't easy for my mother to dress stylishly, but she was very creative. She could turn an otherwise "woegry" hat into a smart item with just a ribbon or scrap of material she had left over from making a dress for a customer.

Sisi always had a worldview. She enjoyed reading newspapers, but she couldn't afford to buy them. When she found part-time work at Morgan's Pharmacy, she brought home discarded newspapers from the day before. If there wasn't a newspaper available, she listened to the BBC on our battery-powered radio. If she couldn't afford to replace the battery, we learned to stay away from her (she didn't have much of a sense of humor). We, however, got a glimpse of how secure and proud a woman she was when my sister Olive was chosen to represent Sierra Leone at the Commonwealth Games in Jamaica in 1966.

It was not uncommon for my father to show up out of the blue. During those challenging days, my mother was valiantly trying to hold the family together, but she would never get into an argument in front of us over money. She was always very respectful of her own mother and us children, and she avoided raising her voice in public.

In retrospect, I can see how my mother was becoming a frustrated, angry, and often depressed woman.

The Unexpected

Many years later, when I returned to Sierra Leone in 2006, I was able to examine the birth certificates of our family—and was I ever in for a shock! I discovered that my grandmother never married. She birthed four children, but not one of them had the same father. My mother was her only daughter.

I also was surprised to learn that my grandmother didn't really raise my mom. Sisi was sent to live with relatives, who treated her as cheap labor. Her daily life as a child consisted of sweeping floors, washing dishes, and cleaning fish. Even at the tender age of six or seven, she would be taken to Freetown, not as a special outing, but to help carry heavy goods back home. While her brothers went to school, it is unclear how much formal education she actually received and how much was self-taught.

I didn't know it then, but these two women were the "ten and two" on my "steering wheel." Grandma Constance was the master of situational ethics and had an endless supply of compassion. In her world, things were colored "gray." She was the refuge you sought for comfort.

Sisi was the rudder: careful, deliberate, focused, unwavering. Her world was marked with definite margins of black and white. There was very little gray. She was the beacon you sought for clarity.

I got into trouble at school one day. A classmate, whose father was a college professor, had given her a fountain pen with a "gold" nib. Everyone oohed and aahed over it. As I reached for it for closer examination, the pen fell, tip first. The resulting distorted pen tip was only partially mirrored by the sharp twist of the horror I felt in my stomach.

"Look what you did! You have to replace it," shrieked my classmate.

We hadn't eaten for three days. How was I ever going to solve this?

Sensing something amiss, Mama finally cornered me. "What's wrong?" she asked, searching my face so she could look directly into my eyes.

When I told her, she became very quiet. I knew I was in deep trouble. The next morning I was deliberately slow in preparing for school. I could try feigning being sick, or perhaps dodge school altogether. But where would I hide? My thoughts were interrupted by Mama ordering me to her room. "Pull my portmanteau [suitcase] out from under the bed," she said.

This was a sacred item. No one ever touched this suitcase without permission. She reached in and pulled out an Le 2.0 note. "Go pay for the pen," she instructed as she handed it to me. "We won't tell your mother, but pray that none of us gets sick. This is the only money I have kept for many years in case one of you became very ill."

Now I felt even more sick to my stomach! This was our emergency fund. Even no food for three days did not qualify as an emergency.

Sisi's verdict would have been swift, clear, and actionable: "We don't touch other people's property," as she laid the switch deftly on my behind.

CHAPTER THREE

PENNIES AND POSSIBILITIES

In the days of my youth during the 1950s and '60s, people in Freetown didn't go shopping weekly and store their goods in refrigerators. Instead we purchased what was needed, one day at a time. Electricity and refrigeration were available, but we—and most of the people in our town—could not afford either. On average, my mother allotted about six pence for food per day, basically for fish and anything we could not grow. She was a whiz at getting the most for her money. For example, we cooked the greens that grow on sweet potatoes. They were not only healthy, but delicious too.

I may have become worldly wise before my time. When my mother entrusted me with a few pennies to buy some fish, I learned how to haggle and strike the best deal possible. I quickly discovered that if you try to purchase seafood in the morning, the catch is fresh and hanging on a rope for all to see. But at the close of the day, if you walk by the same fish seller, most of the catch is no longer on the rope, but down in a basket that might be swarming with flies.

In Freetown, sunset is always close to 6:00 p.m. because we are so near the equator. So at about 5:30 I would ask a seller, "What are you going to do with all that leftover fish?"

They'd respond with something like, "What is it to you?" or, "I'm going to salt it or smoke it."

Well, I knew that probably wasn't going to happen, because they would have to buy the wood for the fire and stay up all night watching it so the fish didn't burn.

Then I'd suggest, "Well, why don't you sell me some for a penny?" That same quantity would have sold for six pence in the morning.

If the seller agreed, I'd reach into the basket and find fish that were still firm and far enough down not to have been touched by the flies. Then I would run home, delighted with my bargain, and my grandmother would fry my "catch" for supper.

Of course, I tried to approach a different seller each day so they wouldn't catch on to my tricks and chime, "Here comes that one-penny girl!" If I was lucky, I'd bring home a prized snapper, which we all loved.

As simple as that may sound, this was my first training ground; it was where I began learning how to negotiate my way through life.

Kicking the Can

The twenty-eighth of each month was either a dreaded day or one of relief. It was when the stipend from my father was due to arrive. A splendid day it was if the envelope was in the mail. Talk about pressure—my mother had to constantly think out of the box and create some innovative ways to handle the limited cash flow.

I remember how she went to the corner store and opened an account to buy staples such as canned milk and sugar on credit. She confidently told the proprietor, "I will pay you at the end of the month." Since everyone in the neighborhood knew of my father's government position, there was never any hesitation to extend such a privilege.

When the bill came due, she would give me an envelope to pay for last month's supplies, but if it was a little short, she would write a note explaining, "This was all that came in from my husband—and listed the items she needed me to bring home 'for the children.'"

She was always "kicking the can down the road." It was all done out of necessity and the dedication she had to her family. And she didn't just owe the corner grocery store; soon the "credit" grew a life of its own.

Mr. Davies, the pharmacist, lived down the street in a three-story concrete home. I became good friends with his family, especially their son, Jacob. His dad was always buying him subscriptions for the *Peanuts* comic books starring Charlie Brown. Since they were his prized possession, he would never loan them out, so I spent a lot of time at their pharmacy, reading the latest editions of his comics. It became another refuge for me.

One day my mom suggested that I ask Jacob if his father would let us have six cans of "Peak" milk on credit. This credit was very readily extended due to our friendship. Later, however, our friendship became awkward when balances were not paid in full.

Survival Training

In the initial stages, there was trust, but as time went on, my mother became more creative. She would skip paying a particular vendor for a month. If the vendor complained, she would pay them first the following month. Perhaps some of the vendors saw how tirelessly she worked in addition to raising four children and caring for her mother as well.

One such sympathizer was our neighbor who was an entrepreneur herself. She was never rude to my mother; however, one day she sent a bag of raw minnow heads to our home. She knew there had been no food in the house for two days. It was hard to keep anything secret in Freetown. If the neighbors didn't see smoke coming from your kitchen for two or three days, they knew you hadn't been cooking. You were in dire straits. My mother looked at those minnow heads, cried, and threw the bag in the garbage!

Around the house each of us had chores. One of us would sweep the floors, another would make sure there was always enough water, and by default, I was the one who ventured to the open markets since I always came home with good deals.

Later, when the time came for me to strike out on my own, my family didn't worry about whether or not I could survive. They had seen my negotiating skills, and their expectations for me were high. They were convinced I would be a success.

If they knew the real me, however, they would have known that when challenges present themselves, first I go into panic mode, and then I explore the possibilities. Next I become emotional, and perhaps even shed a tear or two. But finally I apply every ounce of energy to accomplish the task. With me it was always *do or die!* This set the mold early for problems I would face in the future. The die was cast.

The Green Light

As a senior government official, duty often required my father to travel to Freetown but leave the same day to return to his station. But even when he was in town, his visits were becoming less and less frequent. Despite his long absences, I longed to see my father. If I saw his car parked on the street, I would leave a note on his windshield, "Glena was here. How long are you in town?" I was praying he would stop at the house for a visit.

PENNIES AND POSSIBILITIES

During my middle school years, my best friend Rachel and I loved to walk to the library and check out as many books as we could carry. Television had not yet come to Sierra Leone. We were both avid readers, our minds traveling to faraway places, discovering much about the world and life. At home, if I ever did anything wrong, my worst punishment was hearing the words, "You're not going to the library today!" This was the perfect chance to try out my newly learned deception: "I'm going to Rachel's. She borrowed my book, and I need it for homework." And off I would go, not to Rachel's house, but to the library or to Jacob's to read comic books.

The library was located not too far from the government building where my father had his office. Rachel had spotted his car, and I said, "Let's go see him."

Even though his visits home were becoming rarer, I was so proud of the fact that my dad was situated on the sixth floor of that large building and had a big window with a view overlooking the city. Outside his office door was a small gadget with two lights, red and green, and a button to push. But first you had to write a note stating who you were and the reason for the visit.

I just printed one word: "Glena" and dropped it in the box.

Sure enough, the green light lit up. The door opened, and I walked in, wearing my school uniform. He was standing with three men, hunched over a big desk looking at some plans. Obviously, I was disturbing his day, and he just uttered one word: "What?"

Sheepishly, I replied, "Well, I knew you were here, and I just wanted to say hello."

He muttered a brief, "Well, make sure you get home okay."

Although I was proud of my father's sixth-floor office, my real reason for going there was to see him and ease my anxiety about his unexplained long absences from home.

The Dreaded O-Levels

When I reached the final year of high school, the biggest event was taking the General Certificate of Education (GCE) tests—called the Ordinary or "O-Levels" exams and the equivalent of the SAT and ACT in the United States—and learning the results.

The tests were given over a fixed designated period and divided by subject matter. One session was geography, the next math, then science, history, and so on. Out of thirteen subject areas, one had to pass six or seven for matriculation to any Sierra Leone college. It was a huge deal. The examination was administered to the whole of West Africa, not just my school. Ghana corrected Sierra Leone's papers. Nigeria corrected Ghana's, and so forth.

My grandmother always sat in her special seat from which she could see the front and back doors with just a turn of her head. During the tests, when I arrived home each day, she would insist that I come close and then say to me, "Look into my eyes." I don't know how she could "read" me, but she would say, "You did well today."

I would smile and answer, "Yes."

When I came home from the French exam, Mama asked me, "It was hard, wasn't it?"

I had to agree with her and replied, "Kind of."

We were never informed what day the results would be released, but when the scores were in, you'd know it in a hurry by the young people in the streets, running around either dancing for joy or crying in disappointment!

I will never forget "announcement day." I was outside with my toothbrush, standing by the big drum where we collected rain water.

On hearing the news, I threw on my uniform and ran as fast as I could to the school. The way it was set up, students had to stand in a line in front of Mrs. Garber's office—she was the principal—and wait to be invited in and learn the results.

After what seemed an eternity, it was my turn. Mrs. Garber called my name and asked me to take the chair in front of her desk. "Well, Glena. How do you think you did?"

Trying to act calm, but shaking like a leaf on the inside, I answered, "I feel I did my best, and I hope it was okay."

She smiled and gave me the news: "The lowest score you received was in French, a 7. But you passed everything else and earned an 'A2 Distinction' in English."

What a huge relief! One of the biggest thrills happened later that afternoon when they announced the results on the radio, and I heard my name being read on air.

What's Next

Now it was time to give some serious thought about life after high school. Where would I go, and would I be able to study what I was dreaming of?

During my elementary and high school years, a hiatus had occurred in the educational system. When Sierra Leone was a British protectorate, people who qualified didn't think twice about going to our major university, Fourah Bay, and then transferring straight to Cambridge or another prestigious institution in England.

This was common in my father's and grandfather's generation. For example, before I was born, my father received a degree in England, another in Pennsylvania, and a third back in Britain.

But when Sierra Leone gained its independence in 1961, those in the British Commonwealth questioned, "Why should we educate these Africans for free when they can attend their own colleges? If they want independence, so be it!"

Growing up in the middle of this big gap in the educational process presented challenges for my future.

CHAPTER FOUR

DUST ON MY TONGUE

As a young girl, certain events were indelibly etched on my heart and mind. One was a life lesson in compassion and life choices.

In the absence of a formal foster care system, children could be taken in by another family when their own families could not afford to. Although there was no contract, it was understood that they were taken in to serve the family by doing all the household chores in exchange for room, board, and when convenient, some schooling. Some fared well, attended university, and lived lives indistinguishable from the biological children in the household.

Joseph had been taken in by our next-door neighbor, a woman we called Mama Regina. Joseph and Henry were friends and would often play together.

A relative of the family passed away, and Mama Regina and her husband prepared for a short train trip "up country" from Freetown to attend the funeral. Regina had cooked food for the journey and placed it in special, double-layered aluminum containers—with rice on the bottom, soup on the top, and a strap to carry it all. We call this soup, but it's actually a special sauce that takes all day to make.

Regina left some of the food behind so they would have a meal waiting for them when they returned home on Sunday, because there was no market open on that day. In fact, in Sierra Leone most Christians don't cook on Sunday; they prepare everything in advance. There's a popular saying in West Africa: "Don't eat your Sunday soup on Saturday."

When his parents boarded the train, they left Joseph to fend for himself, but they told him, "If you get hungry, just climb up the tree in the backyard and eat some pink apples." Pink apples (*syzygum aqueum*) were a tropical fruit consisting of 81 percent water.

Joseph wasn't sure when they would return, so he propped open a window, went into the pantry, and devoured most of the soup and rice they had left behind. Then he hung out with Henry in the yard.

Sunday afternoon, Regina and her husband returned and unpacked. When they walked into the pantry, they knew immediately someone had disobeyed their rules. They hollered, "Joseph, come here!" At first he denied tampering with the window.

They tried to warm up what was left of the soup, but it had spoiled. Joseph had used his bare hands to gorge himself and evidently contaminated the food.

With guilt weighing heavy on his mind, Joseph finally confessed. Not only did they beat the lad within an inch of his life with a switch, his parents threw water on him and beat him some more. Then they waited until he had stopped crying and started all over again.

Mama heard all this bedlam and asked, "What's going on?"

We told her, "He stole food that wasn't his."

When things calmed down, she asked us to go and get Joseph. "Why did you steal the soup?" Mama wanted to know.

"Because I was hungry," he replied.

"So you know what it is to be hungry?" said Mama.

"Yes," he answered.

"So when you were eating the soup, did you realize that your mom and dad would be coming back and they would need to eat? You knew it was Sunday, and there would be no other place for them to find food."

Joseph started sobbing again; he hadn't thought that far ahead.

Then Mama told him, "You are a good boy at heart, but you have to rethink this and be responsible for your actions. The reason you were punished is that you have big eyes. You saw the opportunity, and you ate practically all the food instead of just taking some. That's why you got into trouble." Then she counseled, "They didn't beat you because you stole food; it was because you ruined a good meal and deprived everyone else of the food."

Mama's message stuck with me: *Your personal adversity does not excuse the choices you make.* My grandmother's words of wisdom helped me to understand her deep compassion—even for her brother's son, Henry. She knew he had no future if he remained where he was, so she risked her own well-being by bringing him with her when she came to live with her daughter, my mom.

I learned at Mama's feet that even within the limitations of one's adversity, there is still room to help others.

A Steel Resolve

My mother had a steel resolve that I admired. Her brothers all held responsible jobs in business and government. Women were treated differently, and my mom had no more than what I suspect was a formal fourth grade equivalent—but you would have had to be a wizard to know it.

Even though my mother loved her mother, when it came time to care for her, it was only natural for her to think, *Here you are and*

I am willing to welcome you into my home and feed you, but then you bring another mouth to the table, Henry. Why was more being asked of me? I already have a household to feed! But somewhere deep inside she was a titan with steel resolve and determination. She thought, *Whatever you ask of me, I am going to do, as long as I have breath in my body.*

The "School Leaving Dance"

I was the shortest of the three girls, but I had large feet, and mine had grown two sizes more than my sisters. My shoes were also hand-me-downs, and when I would complain, "My feet are too big for these," Sisi would just reply, "Manage. Manage."

We sometimes used what is called soda-soap to wash our clothes, which left them worse for wear. A mixture of lye and oil, it often bleached out some of the color of our clothes. If there was a little extra money, we could splurge and buy a laundry detergent called "Surf." This was a luxury.

I completed high school at the age of fifteen, and Sisi tried to make an outfit for the "School Leaving Dance" out of one of the dresses that had been handed down from Olive to Gloria. It had a blue can-can skirt, and Sisi embellished it with some multilayered taffeta netting, stiffening material, extra frills, and ruffles.

I chose not to attend the dance, however. My excuse: "My shoes are far too tight!"

Decades later, I would laugh long and hard as I listened to a comedienne joke about her prom dress. "Who shot a couch and made you a dress?" she claims someone asked her, referring to her homemade outfit.

Mine was that kind of dress.

A Shoulder to Cry On?

When the monthly stipend from my father was reduced, Sisi took her case to my dad's sister, who also lived in Freetown.

"What am I going to do?" my mother asked her. "How can I raise the children on so little money?"

At first, her sister-in-law was extremely supportive. She would cry with my mother at the thought of what we were going through.

Then one day my mother heard that my father was in town . . . but he had not come home. After all, there were not that many black Vanguards in town—and none with the license plate C48.

As it turned out, he had been seen leaving his sister's house for several days. When my mom went to investigate, she discovered another woman in the home who was my father's "friend."

Sisi quickly put two and two together, and, in her anger, later cried to Mama, "Those people are going to hell, because they're all in this conspiracy together."

When my mother confronted my dad's sister, she just threw up her hands and responded, "What am I supposed to do? After all, he is a man!"

Sisi learned that her husband was not just a philanderer, but he also had fathered two other children, something I would find out much later. Needless to say, the relationship with her sister-in-law quickly soured.

My mother faced a dilemma. If she asked for a divorce, we would all be homeless. Since my father paid the rent and gave her those few Leones each month, she stifled her sorrow and put up with him whenever he came home. She kept my father's infidelity hidden from us. The facts were heartbreaking for my mom, but she never confirmed whatever we suspected.

Eyes in the Rearview Mirror

One day as I was walking in town, I saw a four-door black sedan parked on the side of a dirt road that looked quite familiar. Could it be? Was my father in town? My heart began to leap for joy as I inched closer. Sure enough, I could make out the license plate: C48.

Then I froze as I watched the two people in the front seat locked in a passionate embrace, kissing! The woman looked young enough to be my older sister.

Next I saw the eyes of my father in his rearview mirror, and my heart sank. Suddenly the engine roared, and the Vanguard took off with tires spinning—stirring up a trail of dirt that literally sprayed over my body. I could feel the dust on my tongue.

The nightmare of him speeding away stayed with me. During the succeeding years, I would often wake up in the middle of the night plagued with this memory and feel that unpleasant taste of dust on my tongue.

It was a recurring dream that I didn't share with anyone. But after he passed away, I finally admitted to myself, "It doesn't matter anymore." He had definitely left his mark, though.

Father and Son

My brother, Ian, is ten years younger than me, and the last time my father ever slept under the same roof with us for an extended period of time was when Ian started walking. From that time on, my dad rarely returned home.

I missed him for many reasons, not the least being that whenever he was around, life seemed better. Dad would put money on the table to buy food. If he was eating, so was everyone else.

My father never filed for divorce because at that time in Sierra

Leone, if you had children, there had to be a valid reason for wanting a divorce, and he had none. My mother had done everything he asked of her; she was faithful and took care of the family. So he just gradually made his exit and lived his own life. Irreconcilable differences wasn't yet an acceptable reason for divorce.

A few years later, without telling anybody, I took my brother to my dad's office. His car was in the parking lot, so I knew he was there, but Ian never remembered ever laying eyes on him.

Once again, I wrote my name and dropped it in the box. The two of us walked into his office, and there were some other men in the room with him. Ian turned to me and asked, "Which one is he?"

I whispered, "He's the tall one in the middle."

This time my dad was very cordial. He must have experienced many emotions seeing the son he sired becoming a fine young man.

I have often thought, *What characteristics have I inherited from my mother—and what from my father?*

I believe I inherited from my mom an indomitable spirit that reflects the attitude, "Whatever you ask of me, I will do." I watched her act out the adage, "Do what you can for the present while waiting for what you really want."

Though my father never allowed anyone to dictate his path in life, he had high expectations for himself and others. He would say repeatedly, "Whatever is worth doing is worth doing well." So from him, I possess the ability to see opportunities and possibilities instead of barriers.

I maintain that this is a great inheritance.

CHAPTER 5

TURNING POINTS

There's one question I've been asked more times than I can recount: "Glena, when did you decide to become a doctor? What made you decide on this profession?"

Actually several pivotal moments in my childhood became the catalysts that led to my decision. One of these was when I was around twelve years old. I was relaxing on the small balcony of our house on Upper Waterloo Street, watching some boys who were playing soccer in the street below. Suddenly, a scene unfolded that jarred me into action.

Just down the street lived a rather well-to-do woman who resided in a lovely house with a fenced-in yard, an impeccable garden, and a gate that was always locked. She had a vicious dog, which meant if kids were playing with a ball that bounced into her yard, they couldn't retrieve it, for fear of their lives.

Well, the inevitable happened. The soccer ball sailed over the fence, and one brave boy, thinking that the dog was asleep in the sun, quietly climbed into the yard, retrieved the ball, and was about to make a hasty retreat. Suddenly, the dog jumped up and grabbed him by his buttocks and wouldn't let go.

Immediately I knew the kid was in trouble and, without thinking,

I sprang into action. Rushing to the scene and fending off the snarling animal, I could see that the boy's skin and muscle had been torn away and blood was gushing out. I had never seen a tourniquet applied, but something told me to tear off a piece of cloth and tie it around the open wound.

Somehow I managed to pull the shocked boy out to the street, where I hailed a taxi, yelling to the driver, "Hurry! Take us to the Connaught Hospital"—which was located not far away. On our arrival they immediately stitched him up.

When I left the emergency room and started for home, the cab driver was outside waiting for me. "You can pay me now," he said. But since I didn't have any money, I just darted down a side street and ran for home.

I relived again and again that rescue, but I was surprised by the reaction of the adults in the emergency room. They kept saying to me, "You saved this kid's life. How does someone your age have the sense to do what you did?" I was on to something. If one act could bring so much praise my way, then being a doctor would be a lifelong celebration.

The Doctor's Kids

In a city like Freetown, it is not uncommon to find families rich or poor living side by side—often on the same street.

Not far from us was the home of Dr. Cole, a medical doctor who became a friend of our family's. One day he approached my mother and asked, "There are days when I have to rush into surgery and don't have time to take my children to school. I'm wondering if your girls, Glena and Gloria, could walk with them?"

Sisi happily agreed. With this new responsibility, she was certain I wouldn't dawdle in the morning as I was apt to do, and we wouldn't be late for school.

As a teenager I remember walking up the steps of their beautiful home and being welcomed in. Gloria and I, dressed in our school uniforms, would stand by the dining room table watching them eat. One of the kids (who were both younger than us) would ask, "Mommy, can I have some Weetabix instead of bacon?"

What was in that box? I wondered. It had to be something special.

Next they would pour fresh milk from a pitcher into whatever came out of that Weetabix box. Many days, Gloria and and I would watch wide-eyed as they were served a plate of sizzling bacon or sausage. Even the aroma was delicious! But not once did the parents invite us to join them; they just assumed we had eaten our breakfast at home.

At that young, impressionable age, what I saw was a family that lived well. How does one get to live like that? I could only imagine. One could hope; one could dream . . . dreaming was easy.

So I started dreaming and thinking, *If I could have a life like that, what would it take?* It surprised me that I wanted such a life, but the thoughts lingered.

One of my favorite library books was *Gone with the Wind*, where Scarlett O'Hara dramatically says, "As God is my witness, I'll never go hungry again." I could relate to that.

One day, as Dr. Cole was getting up from the table, he told me and Gloria, "When you walk with the children, please make sure that you hold their hands and walk on the curbside of the street so they are away from the traffic."

The meaning of his words did not escape me. We were potentially disposable body guards. Then it hit me: *They are doctor's children; they are valued. And if I become a physician and have a son or daughter, they will also be valued.*

All this danced in my head, becoming the concrete in the foundation of my thoughts.

Since in my heart of hearts I knew I wanted to be a doctor, I found myself filling my mind with anything pertaining to medicine. At the library, I was drawn to gross anatomy books, with drawings that showed every layer of the human body, inside and out. I especially loved to read about diseases and would wile away the hours, dreaming of cures.

Shocking Words

Perhaps the greatest impetus to me choosing a path for my future took place in my childhood home.

One night my father came to our home very late. My younger brother, Ian, was about three years old at the time. The only bedroom upstairs was where I slept with my two sisters. Ian usually slept with Sisi, because he often fell asleep on Mama's bed. Initially this was were we all congregated to hear Mama tell stories, usually scary ones.

As we got older, our bedroom was the place to be. We would share stories, munching on peanuts and laughing. Ian would often sneak upstairs and spend the night with us.

This particular evening we heard a huge commotion taking place at the foot of the stairs. It was my father, and we listened to him shouting, "Glena, Gloria, Olive! Come down here now!"

We recognized his voice immediately and cautiously made our way downstairs. He ordered us to stand against the wall.

My grandmother was a very soft and gentle person. She often retired to her room in the early evening for the night. You'd rarely see her again until the next morning. But this evening she, too, was standing there, almost cowering in the doorway of her room. My 6'2" father towered over my mom, who is only 4'11" tall.

Then he remembered he had a fourth child, and called for Ian. By his tone I knew there was big trouble ahead, but I had no idea what to expect.

Speaking to us and not my mother—as if she was either stupid or deaf—he angrily blurted out words I cannot erase from my memory: "Tell her I will f_____ anybody I want."

I watched my mom shrink, not only in body, but in spirit. She seemingly had no reserve or strength to fight back. His words were hurtful and humiliating, especially when said in the presence of her children and her mother.

I wondered, *What is wrong with this picture? Is it because she is so small and he is so big? Is it simply the fact that he is a man and she is a woman?*

Surely this couldn't be the reason, especially since I had seen Dr. Cole treat his wife and children with such love, dignity, and respect. He even wanted to provide human shields for his valued children.

The woman my father was seeing was the matron at the Connaught Hospital, and he appeared to be highly impressed by her profession. To make matters worse, he concluded his tirade by looking at my mother and saying, "And she is not woegry like you!"

He then dismissed us and walked out of the house. My innocence was shattered, and I didn't sleep a wink the rest of the night. I kept tossing and turning, thinking, *My father is so powerful—and my mother seems so* powerless!

The only conclusion I could come up with was that if you had enough money, you could do whatever you want.

My father was the person we depended on for rent and food. He controlled the purse. And once again, new thoughts danced in my head. I decided, *I will forever control my own purse, and be the keeper of its keys*—and I concluded that earning my own way in life was the only way to obtain a key.

In addition I determined that no one would ever humiliate me the way my father had belittled my mother in front of us, his own flesh and blood. He was not a doctor, and I had noted that doctors valued their children. Not only did they save lives, they valued lives.

In that moment I knew I had to become a doctor. I had to find a way to save myself, my children, my country.

I now had big dreams.

Jacob's Bon Voyage

In Sierra Leone, at that time, the idea of a young woman becoming a physician seemed far-fetched—especially since there was no medical school in the country. You had to leave home to receive such an advanced education. In addition the curriculum for girls was not on par with that of boys.

For example, at my girl's school there was a general science course that lumped physics, chemistry, and biology into one unit. But at the Prince of Wales school (primarily for boys), these were three separate courses.

For young men, traveling to England to further their education was a big deal, but it was not a consideration for young women.

For example, even before he completed high school, my friend Jacob, the son of Mr. Davies, the pharmacist, knew his family planned to send him to Great Britain to continue his schooling. I remember as if it were yesterday the announcement that he would be taking the S.S. *Apapa,* a noted steamer in the Elder Dempster Line that made regular runs between West Africa and Liverpool. My father had boarded the same ship as a young man when he studied in England.

Jacob's family invited me to attend a "bon voyage" party on the ship just before it sailed. Jacob's mother told me, "Be sure you wear white gloves and a fancy dress."

My mom could make the dress, but there was no money for the gloves—and Sisi grumbled at me for even *wanting* to attend the event. She was concerned that I was aligning myself with people who were out of my league.

To make matters worse, I knew there was a fee to enter the area where the ship was docked in the quay. It included a tour of the ship. Every time I saw Mrs. Davies, she would inquire, "Do you have your dress and gloves yet?"

Eventually I had to tell her the truth: "My father hasn't sent our money this month, so it looks doubtful that I will be able to make it."

Thankfully Mrs. Davies kindly said, "Don't worry, I will pay the fee for the tour. I just want you to be there."

Somehow, some way, Sisi finally came up with the white gloves, and I was thrilled to be able to see Jacob off.

Deep down I felt sorry for my mother. Our quarrels were usually the result of her saying things like, "You always look beyond what you are capable of." I, on the other hand, didn't see the harm in dreaming.

In hindsight I can certainly understand why she felt that way. When she married a bright, college-bound man, she believed her life would greatly improve and they would grow old together. But in reality just the opposite happened.

I was in awe when I walked on to that beautiful steamship and saw how people who had the money to travel lived. There were hand-rubbed decks and highly polished rails. I learned that the passengers could sit at the captain's table at least once during the voyage and feast on pheasant or roast beef—a far cry from the chicken wings I munched on at home. This was truly another world I briefly entered as I bid farewell to my friend Jacob.

It only stirred new yearnings of a life I could only dream of.

A Woman Doctor?

When the opportunity presented itself, I asked Dr. Cole's wife, who was a midwife, "If you are not a midwife or a matron, what else can you do in medicine?"

I already knew the answer, but I wanted to hear it from her lips: "You can always become a doctor," she told me. "You can't get any higher than that."

This made perfect sense to me. *Every day somebody will get sick, thereby ensuring a continuous demand for a doctor's services,* I mused.

But a *female* doctor? Then I heard that the woman who became the mayor of Freetown was also a physician. On learning this news, it cemented my conviction that I was on to something.

Because of the grades I received on my O-Levels, I was allowed to enroll as a full-time student at the Prince of Wales school and take what was called the "Five-Attached" class in science. The "five" meant that it was the equivalent of the fifth year of high school. I could not attend college right away as some of the the courses such as General Science were not acceptable for matriculation at college.

I was now seventeen years old. I worried, *What about my dreams? Where is the open door I can walk through?*

CHAPTER SIX

TIRED OF CHICKEN WINGS

What a mess! Two huge trucks pulled up in the front of our school and literally dumped hundreds of books in the middle of the yard.

They were a gift from the United States Information Service, a branch of the U.S. Embassy in Sierra Leone. They had decided to donate their old books to our library.

The principal told the students, "Go outside and pick up as many as you can and put them on the shelves. We will sort and catalog them later."

I did my part, but there was one particular title that grabbed my attention. It was *I Know Why the Caged Bird Sings*, the autobiography of Maya Angelou. I wouldn't let it out of my hand. When I had a chance, I found a quiet spot in a corner of the school where no one could see me, and I began reading.

I loved the story where Maya wrote how she and her brother didn't think too highly of Reverend Howard Thomas, the presiding elder over their church's district. When he came to visit, he would be invited to Sunday dinner at their house—always taking the best parts of the chicken and not leaving much for the kids.

I laughed and laughed when Maya took great satisfaction during a service when a member of the congregation, Sister Monroe, became so overcome by his sermon that she ran to the pulpit and, catapulted by emotion, literally knocked the preacher's dentures out of his mouth.

My imagination ran away with me, because I could identify with parts of the book as it related to our own family. I was so engrossed that by the time I finished reading, it was dark, and I thought, "Oh, I'll be in trouble when I get home."

The Gift of Food

On Christmas Day in Sierra Leone, families and loved ones don't exchange presents as is the custom in America. Instead everything centers around food. It's the day when the very best meal of the year is prepared—one that represents your family and ethnic tribe.

However, the dish you make is not just for those in your household. The "gift giving" comes in the form of sharing part of this sumptuous meal with others, such as a neighbor or the old, frail man with no visible family nearby. Our mother took this to the extreme. She had us run all over town—first to relatives, neighbors, and friends, and then to people she had borrowed money from, even if she had long repaid them. One year there was *nothing* left of the meal we had labored all day to prepare. When we all finally returned from our delivery errands, we were shocked to find nothing for us. She simply said she had put some sweet potatoes to roast on hot coals. We didn't understand. My sisters and I still talk about it. Despite the fact that many family and friends brought dishes of food to our family as their Christmas present, I went to bed that year holding a grudge.

My fear each year was that the mailman wouldn't deliver our monthly cheque by Christmas Eve so we could buy the ingredients for the festive meal. The main stores closed that day at noon, and

I dreaded the embarrassment my mother would endure if she had nothing to offer.

Even now, I can still see myself impatiently pacing on the street corner, watching the mailman walk from house to house. He could not be persuaded to dig into his bag and rifle through the mail. He had to go in order. I'd sometimes rack up enough courage to ask him, "Do you have anything for us today?" He would just ignore me, and I'd have to wait. What sweet relief when that much-awaited envelope showed up on time!

The End of the Road

Since my mind was made up that I would become a doctor, I knew I'd have to leave my hometown. The colleges there could prepare anyone to become a teacher, a member of the clergy, or a business person, but certainly not a physician.

Since we had been a British protectorate, England was the first place I thought of going to reach my dream. But how could I raise the money to finance such a bold venture?

When I mustered up the courage and told Sisi, "I want to go to England," her reaction was, "To teach?"

This reflected her expectations for me regarding the highest level she thought I could possibly attain.

"No," I responded, "I am going to be a doctor."

"But where on earth will you get the money?" she wanted to know.

"Well," I told her, "I am going to find my father and see if he can help me."

Through her tears, Sisi said, "Glena, you are only looking for disappointment."

My attitude, however, was: *If you don't ask, you don't receive!*

I had no idea where my father was, but asked one of our relatives who knew about the Agriculture Center where he was currently stationed. Reluctantly my mother gave me her last two shillings to pay for my ride there and back.

Perhaps because of naivety or my passion to change my circumstances, I had no fear of traveling across the country alone. My driving force was the fact that I was tired of eating wings instead of chicken breasts; tired of waiting for cheques to arrive; tired of wearing hand-me-down clothes.

I was willing to work hard—and travel that Atlantic Ocean to a land of opportunity.

When the transport van reached the end of the road and let all the passengers off, the driver let me out and asked, "Where are you going?"

I replied, "Please ask that man over there where the Agriculture Center is located."

Following his directions, I reached the compound and inquired, "Which one is the Palmer-Davies house?"

"It's number 2." So that's where I headed. The houseboy let me in with no questions asked.

"What's that you have cooking?" I wanted to know. He fed me; I looked too much like my dad for anyone to doubt I was his child.

"What time will my father be home?" I asked.

 "Since it is Friday, he may be late." He continued, "Mr. Palmer-Davies will either be downtown, or down at the bar."

"Would you please take me there?" I asked.

Sure enough, we found him seated at the bar, chatting with a group of friends. When he spotted me, he paused for a second and then continued talking as if I wasn't there. I'm sure he was racking his brain, wondering, *What's going on here? What is she going to bug me for now?*

Obviously, since I had traveled so far, he knew this must be important. So, without even a "hello," he asked, "Would you like some orange Fanta?"

Until that moment I had only tasted Fanta a couple of times. What a treat to be served a whole bottle!

My father finally said, "Let's go," but he didn't take me back to his house. Instead, we wound up at a woman's home. Apparently my dad hadn't changed.

I can still see the big cast iron pot just outside in the front yard. As I walked past that pot, I knew there was more than chicken wings and drumsticks simmering away.

Inside, the atmosphere was calm and very normal. I was *not* introduced as his daughter, but by my facial features, I'm sure the woman knew.

Bracing myself, I made my case. "I received wonderful grades on my O-Levels and they called my name on the radio." Then I added, "I want to go to England and study to be a doctor."

"Well, I'm sure Princess will help you," he replied, referring to one of his sisters who had been in England for as long as I had been alive. "I will get her to send you the application forms."

Then he took me to his residence, where I slept in the house alone.

When I arose the next morning, there was gift waiting for me. It was three yards of colorful tie-dyed cloth, more than enough for a dress.

I spent my final shilling for the ride back to Freetown. The first question my mother asked on seeing me was, "Did he give you any money?"

"No," I answered, "but he gave me this piece of cloth."

I could see the disappointment written on her face. I was anxious but hopeful.

The Letter That Didn't Arrive

Once more it was time for "mailman anxiety." Every day I waited for the promised letter from my aunt in England containing the university application papers.

When it failed to arrive, I paid a visit to Mrs. Garber, the principal of the girl's school where I had graduated. She said, "You have probably waited too long, because by now most students have already been accepted."

I'm still not sure whether she felt sorry for me or actually needed help at the school, but she offered me a job as an assistant in the science lab. It paid 16 Leones a month, which to me was a huge sum of money.

That term, there was a problem between the Ministry of Education, the teaching staff, and Mrs. Garber. The entire faculty went on strike. Because of this situation, I ended up teaching Geography, Latin, and English, while still working in the lab, all for the same pay. I was not a trained teacher.

Knowing my deep desire to study abroad, Mrs. Garber suggested, "Let's go over to the United States Information Services office and check out some colleges in America. You have other options available to you besides England."

There was a directory with a long list of educational institutions in the U.S., divided by regions: East, Midwest, and West.

The USIS personnel staff and Mrs. Garber were very protective. They cautioned, "You shouldn't consider going to New York or Chicago—those cities are too big and way too dangerous."

Mrs. Garber added, "I would also forget about California—too many hippies!"

So I made a list of possible colleges and wrote down the addresses.

Soon after, Mrs. Garber asked me to go to the Fourah Bay College, which sits high on Mount Aureol in Freetown, to pick up lab materials for our school that had been sent there.

Upon my arrival, I noticed a long line that snaked around the block. In Freetown, when you see a queue that size, you jump in, assuming it is for something special. I did, and someone told me, "It's an exam for people who would like to study in America."

Wow! This was my lucky day!

When I finally reached the front of the line, the man behind the desk called out, "Next! Registration papers, please."

"Sir, I don't have any," I replied.

He looked at me, momentarily agitated, but said, "Okay, here." He handed me a pink form and told me, "Fill this out and you can register on-site. The fee is two shillings."

I froze. "Sir," I quietly responded, "I don't have two shillings."

He reached into his pocket and paid the fee for me. I was shocked. "Tell your parents they can reimburse me later."

I walked into a room full of desks and anxious faces. The attendant placed papers in front of me, and at the top was written "SAT Exam."

I had never heard of such a test. We were in the British system, with totally different evaluations. Unlike studying for the GCE (General Certificate of Education), I experienced no anxiety while taking the SAT as I had no idea of its implications.

To my surprise, it wasn't long before I began receiving letters from colleges in the U.S. saying, "Congratulations. We are the University of (whatever), and this is an invitation to apply to our school."

I quickly forgot about England.

Most of the applications included a required financial information form. Since the conversion to U.S. dollars didn't compute for me, I walked into the bank and asked for their help.

One of the questions was, "What is your household income?"

The banker calculated this, based on the total income of me, my siblings, and mother. It came to a grand total of approximately two hundred dollars a year!

During this time, I used the USIS as my personal office, asking for help from whoever was on duty.

I had narrowed down the invitations to about eight colleges, and I discovered that the cost of colleges in the U.S. was about five thousand dollars a year. Of course, my two-hundred-dollar annual family income didn't make sense, and some of the institutions politely declined my application.

One of the universities actually thought I had made a mistake and changed the decimal to a comma and wrote in $200,000 a year. The attached note read, "If this is correct, kindly initial this change and send it back to us."

I took the document to the bank, and they laughed. "Nobody makes that kind of money in Sierra Leone." So I returned the form, writing out "Two Hundred Dollars" in words, not numbers.

One of the schools wrote, "Considering your financial situation, you will receive a work-study grant, which means you will have to accept employment on campus to make up the difference." The letter was from Carroll College, a private liberal arts school located in Waukesha, Wisconsin, a suburb of Milwaukee.

My heart was beating out of my chest!

CHAPTER SEVEN

TUNNEL VISION

It was Saturday, September 4, 1971, when a wide-eyed nineteen-year-old girl bade good-bye to her family in Freetown and boarded an airplane headed for America. I was the first of my siblings to leave home.

At the arrivals wing of the Milwaukee airport, I saw a sign with my name written on it. Holding it was Bill Guthrie, my soon-to-be foreign student advisor and lifelong friend from Carroll College, who greeted me with a warm welcome and drove me to the campus.

Compared to the crowded upstairs bedroom I shared with my two sisters at 38 Upper Waterloo Street, the dorm seemed spacious; to me it was pure luxury. On Monday I registered for classes and was given my first on-campus job as part of the promised work-study program. It was in the cafeteria, where I would be checking students who were on the meal plan. Later I had a variety of assignments, including sweeping floors and processing mail in the Foreign Students office.

On Sundays I attended church, did my homework, and cleaned my room. It was a day without a set schedule.

Carroll had a large representation of international students, and there also were some black students from around the U.S. Since

I had a crisp British accent, a few on campus thought this was an affectation and gave me a wide berth. This didn't upset or bother me since I had tunnel vision regarding my studies and was only there for one purpose: to study. There was no turning back.

It was a culture shock to hear the conversations in the girls' dorm. Instead of talking about academics, most of the banter centered on movies, fashion, and "boys." I often felt out of place. I had a singular focus: to finish college. Why complicate things? I broke my concentration one day, however, when I overheard two girls discussing "Afro hairdos."

"What kind of Afro do I have?" I asked, interrupting one of them. Without missing a beat, she replied, "That, my dear, is what I call a mess!"

Feeling the Pressure

During the years I worked as a lab assitant in Sierra Leone, I dated Emile Jones, who came from a well-known family. He was headed for life as a clergyman and was studying to become an Anglican priest.

Before leaving for the U.S., his sister took me aside and said, "We are very sure about Emile's commitment to you, but we are not sure about your commitment to him. You are going to America as a woman on your own. Can you give us the reassurance that when you return, you will come back to him?"

I did not reply. Instead, I had a long talk with Emile on our front porch, telling him, "You are the one who speaks about God and our future. If it is His will, we will both know it. But as of now, you don't have any claims on me. So just talk to the Lord about the matter."

"Fair enough," he said. And that's the way we left our relationship.

Now separated by thousands of miles, Emile and I kept up with each other by mail. Other than telling me how much he missed me, he was totally fixated on the ministry. He wrote, "Glena, when I become a pastor, you will be perfect as president of the Women's Union at our church, and you will be able to stay at home with our children."

His words really gave me pause for reflection. At this time during the 1970s, the feminist movement in America was in full swing, and I questioned, *Did I come all this way only to go back and sit in a parsonage owned by the church, lead a ladies' group, and have kids?*

Emile was raised by his aunt since his own mother had died in childbirth. Still, I was somewhat taken aback when I received a letter from her. "Glena," she wrote, "instead of gallivanting around the world, don't you think that sooner or later you should settle down with Emile?" And she let me know that sooner would be preferable.

I took umbrage at the word *gallivanting* since I was not running around globetrotting, but was totally dedicated to chasing a dream.

Emile was persistent in his commitment to the relationship, and eventually we would meet face-to-face again.

An Unexpected Ruling

My first semester at Carroll College was running smoothly until the day I received a notice that caused my world to turn upside down.

Even though I had entered the college on a work-study program, that fall the government changed the rules and sent out notices to every foreign student: "If you are not a citizen of the United States, you cannot work." This translated to not receiving any type of remuneration from the college.

Frightened, I made an appointment to see both my foreign student advisor, Bill Guthrie, and Bruce Cozzini, my academic advisor and chemistry professor. They were as concerned as I was over the ruling, and they did their best to help me any way they could.

The Cozzinis had three children, and Bruce asked, "Would you like to babysit our kids? My wife, Carol, and I like to go to Chicago on the weekends. " He even suggested, "You can bring your laundry and cook if you like."

Since their home was located just down the street from the campus, it was a perfect setup—and it gave me a few much-needed dollars.

Carroll College had a 4-1-4 academic plan, which meant that each course was taught in four months, with a one month break before the next course.

I continued to eat my meals in the cafeteria until the finance manager stopped me on the street and said, "Glena, I've been trying to reach you. Your paperwork is not in order, and you can't eat in the cafeteria until it is cleared up."

Evidently I wasn't the only student with such a problem. The Puerto Rican students were spared the no-work order. Word spread that they had food at the Black House, the de facto international center. My visits were frequent.

Before I knew it, it was time for the second semester, but I wasn't allowed to register because I had outstanding college bills that hadn't been paid.

When the Cozzinis found out the seriousness of my plight, they went to the administration and pleaded my case, saying, "If you don't let her register, how is she going to continue her studies here?"

The college offered me a solution: "Write your father and tell him that he needs to repay all the funds you owe, or you can not remain as a student." I did as they requested, and they mailed the registered letter to the Sierra Leone Ministry of Education, with a copy to my father at the Ministry of Agriculture. Thus, with the prodding of the Cozzinis and with the expectation that my father would pay the money owed, the college allowed me to register, but since I had no income, I couldn't pay the dorm fees.

Bruce and Carol generously stepped in again. "Why don't you come and live with us? The children love you, and so do we."

I happily accepted their gracious invitation and quickly bonded with the family.

A Cheque in the Mail

It was past midterms, and the college still hadn't heard a word from my father. Then came another notice: "Under no circumstances can you continue your education here until all outstanding bills are paid in full by _____." The date they specified was the end of the school year.

During that spring semester, an envelope arrived from Cassius, a young man who had written me my first love letter in Freetown. He, too, had traveled to the States and was a student at Marion College in Indiana (now called Indiana Wesleyan University).

Enclosed was a cheque for twenty-six dollars, with a note that read, "This is for bus fare. Please come and visit me."

It came at a time when I was absolutely penniless, so when I held that cheque in my hand, I sat down and cried, because that very day I had asked God to help me somehow find enough money to purchase some sundries—some very personal—which I desperately needed.

I cashed the cheque, and I never answered Cassius' note. It was the first time in my life I had ever done anything like that, and I felt terrible. I felt ashamed, and so I prayed, "Please, God, I am not spending his money foolishly. I am asking you not to hold this against me." It somehow diminished me, though.

Work! Study! Breathe!

The nights were growing dark earlier, leaves were falling from the trees, but the door remained closed regarding my return to Carroll College. The Cozzinis made one more suggestion. "We think you should consider transferring to the Waukesha campus of the University of Wisconsin." It was a two-year junior college program. "Just go and register!"

In the summer, to make ends meet I began doing many odd jobs for families who lived on Charles Street—mowing lawns, cleaning houses, babysitting, you name it. I even took a part-time job cleaning bathrooms at a nearby hotel. I eventually got a job at Avalon Manor, a senior center in Waukesha, at an hourly wage of $1.65. I could work as many hours as I could physically manage—in the kitchen, serving meals in the dining room, vacuuming, and cleaning residents' bathrooms. The good thing was that all the hours were available in one location. But it was too far to walk, so I rode nine-year-old David Cozzini's bike side-saddle, coasting downhill to Avalon Manor—and walking the bike back home after work. I'm sure I didn't go unnoticed in my white uniform, zipping in and out of traffic.

At the end of the day, I would eat a plate of whatever the residents were having. Then one Saturday, the director of the facility saw me eating and called me over, "Glena, I don't remember you signing up to have your meals deducted from your pay cheque."

"Oh," I replied, "I'm sorry. I didn't know I had to do that. No one told me."

After we disagreed over how much the deductions would amount to, I declined the meal plan. It was back to sardines and crackers! I always carried these staples with me.

I didn't know if my father would come through with the money, but I was still a child with hope. My days were wrapped up in three words: work, study, breathe. Work, study, breathe. Nothing else mattered.

In the process of attempting to register at the two-year junior college, I had to ask Carroll College to release my transcripts. But my request was denied since I still owed them money. The matter was brought to the attention of the Board of Trustees.

A member of the board was a woman named Mrs. Elsie Hanson, who lived two doors down from the Cozzinis. I didn't know it at the time, but she had been watching me from her window for several months. Evidently she was impressed with my work ethic, being both loving and stern with the children and diligently completing every task that was given me by the neighbors on Charles Street.

One day the phone rang while the Cozzinis were out, and a voice said, "You haven't been to church in seven months"—which was true. It was Mrs. Hanson, and she introduced herself. She was a member of the Board of Trustees at Carroll College, but she didn't tell me that right away. Instead she ordered, "Get your white uniform in a pant-suit style instead of a dress and you can pedal home instead of walking your bike—and by the way, that bike is too small for you!"

Mrs. Hanson didn't make suggestions; she "gave orders." At the next meeting of the college board, this woman let her opinion be heard in no uncertain terms: "You agreed to bring this student to the United States on a work-study program, then halfway through the first semester, the government pulled the rug out from under her and left her high and dry. So we have an obligation here." She continued, "I'm not asking you to spend money on a foreigner, but can't you just release her records so she can continue her education?"

Her passionate plea resonated with the board, and I was able to enroll at the University of Wisconsin–Waukesha.

Trusting the Driver

During those days of trials and testing, I drew great comfort by constantly talking with God. The wide-eyed, naive girl was changing into a guarded woman, fearful yet clinging to my childlike faith that allowed me to envision my life's journey akin to riding a bus.

You depend on the driver to take you to your destination because he knows the way. He may take you on a detour that you don't like or didn't expect. The trip may be long and tiring, and the scenery may not always be picturesque. But the driver knows the bends and curves of the road and where he is headed. And you have the inner peace that you will arrive safely.

So I asked God to take the wheel. If I didn't like the scenery out of one window, I could look out the other side.

What an unforgettable journey my heavenly Father had planned!

CHAPTER EIGHT

BIG DOORS SWING ON SMALL HINGES

During my first semester at Carroll College, one Sunday morning I was taking a walk, breathing in the fresh Wisconsin air. Suddenly a big black car pulled up beside me.

The woman in the passenger seat rolled down her window and asked, "We're looking for a foreign student from Sierra Leone named Glena Davies. Do you happen to know her?"

My mind was spinning: *Had I done something wrong? Who are these people? Why are they asking about me?*

My first instinct was to be evasive. But then I said, "May I ask why you are looking for her?"

The woman explained, "We are from the First Baptist Church of Waukesha, and I am a graduate of Carroll." She continued, "Every year we call the foreign student office and ask for the names of the foreign students. We invite them to a special luncheon to share with them the culture and traditions of the Midwest—and she is the only one we have not been able to contact."

Feeling a little more comfortable, I presented my biggest smile and announced, "I am Glena." Then I asked, "How long is the program?"

"Oh, it's just a couple of hours, but we would love for you to join us at the church service first," the woman answered.

I agreed to go, but I told them I needed to run back and pick up my books first.

When I did, I quickly asked a couple of students in my dormitory, "Do you know about a First Baptist Church in Waukesha?"

They said, "Oh, yeah," which immediately put my mind at ease.

When I returned to the car, the couple was still waiting for me.

"We are Ken and Doris Steele, and it is so good to meet you," Ken said as he opened the door to the back seat and helped me in.

I had no idea at the time, but this meeting would become one of the most pivotal moments of my new life.

A Coat in the Cold

After the luncheon, Doris suggested, "If you have the time, we'd like to give you a tour of Pewaukee, where we live." Pewaukee is a village just north of Waukesha. Since the only America I had seen up to that point was the few blocks around Carroll College and the route to Avalon Manor, I jumped at the opportunity.

I felt very comfortable with the Steeles. Ken had done plenty of farming and, like my dad, had a lot of knowledge about agriculture. Doris enjoyed sewing, just like my mom. Plus her father had been a physician. This gave us plenty to talk about.

After driving around the countryside, they took me to their home. Ken and Doris asked me dozens of questions about my past and future, and they commented on my fervor and zeal to become a doctor. As we were talking in her kitchen, I noticed that her spice rack was rather disorganized. I felt comfortable enough to ask, "How about if we straightened that up?"

We tackled the job together—and the next thing I knew it was seven o'clock in the evening. Time had flown by!

Doris went out of her way to show me kindness beyond measure. She noticed I was wearing a pair of tennis shoes, but no socks. Soon a pair of nylons, some oranges, and other small gifts appeared in my campus post office box. These acts of generosity happened again and again.

I must have really stood out in Wisconsin, wearing my African clothes. Since I didn't own a pair of boots or a coat, when winter set in, I literally ran from one building to the next. One cold day, the Dean of Women called me to her office. She simply ordered me to her car. We drove to a nearby shopping mall where she bought me a brand-new, warm, thick coat. I couldn't believe it—and I was so grateful.

Not long after, on a brutal winter day, I saw an Hispanic woman shivering at a bus stop, huddled with her children, who all seemed worse off than I had ever been. She wasn't wearing a coat, so I took off the one that had been gifted to me and handed it to her. I didn't feel the blast of bitter cold air, because I was warm on the inside. I was reliving Mama's teachable moment: "Personal adversity is no excuse from moral obligations."

Two weeks later, Doris Steele picked me up on the way to church—and to my amazement, she presented me with a beautiful coat she had made herself. Once again, I felt that the Lord was watching over me.

Every time the Steeles invited me into their home, I did whatever I could to help them. Our friendship blossomed to the point that soon I was calling them "Mom and Dad."

An "X" on the Employment Form

During my second year of college, after transferring to the University of Wisconsin–Waukesha and living with the Cozzinis, they told me of their decision to move to California.

Panic immediately set it. Not only would I miss them, but where would I live?

Once again angels stepped into the void. Doris and Ken, on hearing the news, said "Glena, why don't you come and stay at our house?"

There was no rent to be paid, and no money exchanged hands. I was living free of charge, and I thanked God every day for His many blessings. I will never forget their openhearted kindness.

In the summer of 1973, to earn a few extra dollars, I found a part-time job at a bakery in Pewaukee. Their claim to fame was that they made the best wedding cakes.

I must have looked like a disheveled mess when I rode a bicycle to the store and told the owner, "If you give me a job, I will do anything!"

"Will you wash dishes?" he asked.

When I nodded yes, he took out an employment form and placed an "X" on the signature line. "Put this mark on that line." He didn't ask me to sign my name, so I assumed he didn't think I could.

The man must have thought I fell off a truck, but I didn't say a word, not wanting to rock the boat. Instead I satisfied his ignorance and placed an "X" on the line.

He walked me to the back of the store and said, "You can start by washing the baking pans." Then he gave me a tour of the building. Perhaps to inspire me, he remarked, "See that fellow over there? He used to wash dishes, but now he makes flowers out of cake icing. Some day you'll be like him."

I not only cleaned the grubby pans, I shined them with steel wool. It wasn't part of my duties to clean the grease trap, but I faithfully did that unpleasant task every other day, rain or shine.

My employer noticed my extra efforts and commented, "It looks like you are going to rise very fast in this company. If you want a job again next summer, just let me know."

Fall was arriving. Here I was, thousands of miles away from home, with no idea how or where I would continue my education. Just like my ancestors who stood on the shore in Nova Scotia praying, "Whatever it takes, I am going to get on that boat for a better life," I kept assuring myself, "I know I can make it on my own here."

My Advocates

Unbeknownst to me, a group of men and women who had more than a fleeting concern for this girl from Sierra Leone somehow had been drawn together. The group included Mrs. Hanson, the Cozzinis, the Steeles, and a growing number of individuals at First Baptist Church, where I was now regularly attending.

Without my knowledge, these "advocates" held a meeting to discuss options for my future, even putting out feelers to other colleges on my behalf.

Then one evening at the Steele's home, the phone rang and the caller asked for me. On the line was a woman who said, "I am from the admissions office at Wilmington College in Ohio. We know you did not apply to our school, but we have come to know that your academic record is stellar and your work ethic is excellent. You seem like the kind of student who would make us proud."

My jaw dropped. For a moment I was speechless.

She continued, "We are offering you a full scholarship, and you will be part of a work program that has nothing to do with the federal government."

I had no clue how they had heard of my state of affairs until I learned later that my "angels" had talked with one of my former professors, Bill Guthrie, who had left Carroll College and was now head of the English department at Wilmington.

The End of the Road?

Two years later I walked through the graduation line to receive my Bachelor of Science degree, with a major in both biology and chemistry.

In the dorms that spring, the students in my field were constantly abuzz, asking each other, "Where are you applying to medical school?"

On "career days," representatives from various universities set up booths to promote their programs. I was more than interested, but one after another told me, "Well, you have to be a U.S. citizen."

That left me out. Did this mean I would have to return to Freetown and teach biology? If that were the case, I would consider myself a failure. I would simply be fulfilling my mother's expectation that I would become a teacher. I had come too far to settle for that.

Then I spoke with the representative from Ohio State University. They had a master's program in Public Health and Preventative Medicine. As I scoured through the brochure, there was nothing stating that American citizenship was required. In fact, the main purpose of the program was to train students from many underdeveloped nations because of their dire need for improved public health.

Without wasting any time, I applied and was accepted. To my delight I learned that everything was paid for—including room, board, and textbooks. I would also be a teacher's assistant and receive a small stipend.

At OSU I met students from Brazil, Indonesia, Nigeria, and many other countries. But I had absolutely no desire to return to West Africa at this time without securing a medical degree. My only goal was to somehow be admitted to a U.S. medical school.

Eventually I finished the course work for a master's degree in Epidemiology and Public Health. All that was left was to present a thesis, and the degree from OSU would be mine.

One day there was an unexpected bonus. Just before leaving campus, one of the secretaries came up to me in the hallway and asked, "You are Glena Davies, aren't you?"

When I answered yes, she said, "Everybody else has stopped by to pick up their stipend money, but you have never collected yours."

That's how naive I was on how the system worked.

She continued, "Please visit my office, and I'll give you the cheque."

The amount was for just over a thousand dollars—the most money I had ever possessed! My heart started beating overtime, and I thought I was the richest girl in the world.

Willing to Crawl

Every summer during my years at Wilmington and Ohio State, I returned to Pewaukee and stayed with the Steeles. They welcomed me with open arms, and I considered it my home in America.

I continued to correspond with my old boyfriend, Emile, from Freetown. He wrote that he would be visiting his two brothers who had moved to Canada, and he begged me to make the trip to see him. I did—taking a bus from Milwaukee to Toronto.

His brothers drove me from the bus station to the airport, and the moment I saw Emile step off the plane, I knew in my heart of hearts that not only was marriage not a consideration for me at that moment, but this was not the man I was going to marry.

We were on two different paths for our future. His was to be an Anglican clergyman; mine was in medicine.

For several months I had often awakened to a recurring thought: "Help your future. Give destiny a push."

With every bone in my body, I believed in what destiny had in store for me. If there was a setback, I would compartmentalize it—and either deal with the situation, forget it, or put the challenge on a shelf and tie a ribbon around it for future reference or resolution.

No matter what, I would become a doctor, even if I had to crawl all the way.

As my life unfolded, my mind would often return to that Sunday morning when I was stopped on the street by total strangers and invited to a luncheon at a church in Waukesha, Wisconsin.

It continues to remind me that big doors really *do* swing on small hinges.

CHAPTER NINE

BEHIND THE SCENES

While I was still a student at the University of Wisconsin–Waukesha, one day I was ironing when the phone rang at the Steele residence. After Doris listened to the caller for a while, I heard her say, "I don't know, but I'll ask her."

She put her hand over the receiver and said, "It's Bob Kern, an important member of our Board of Trustees at church, and he wants to talk with you."

Even though I had become a member of First Baptist in Waukesha and helped in the nursery on Sundays, I had never met the gentleman—but evidently he knew about me.

"My wife and I have to fly to Japan tomorrow, and I'm wondering if you could come over and stay with my mother while we are gone." asked Mr. Kern. "It will only be for a week."

"Let me talk with Mrs. Steele," I responded.

When I did, she encouraged me to say yes, which I did.

Two hours later, Mr. Kern picked me up and drove me to his home.

The houses in America were nothing like the one I had grown up in. There, timing was everything. I had perfected my morning dance. Standing by the rain barrel, I would brush my teeth until I could no longer resist the call of nature. Then and only then I would enter the latrine—that place where cockroaches waited under the wooden box with a hole cut out in its center. They lurked just out of sight but made their presence known by sweeping their feelers over your butt cheeks. "Speedy delivery" was my plan.

Now, at the Kern home, Mr. Kern introduced me to his mother, a petite woman with a welcoming smile. Her first words were, "I'm going to fix some dinner. What would you like? Steak?"

Mrs. Kern interrupted. "Excuse me while I go upstairs and put a couple of things on the bed for you. Your room will be the second on the right."

Later, when I walked into the bedroom, there was a new pair of pajamas and two silver bracelets—just for me. Sinking my feet into that deep, plush carpet, I felt like royalty.

Mr. Kern and his wife gave me a brief tour of the house, including a small chapel adorned with stained glass windows. "This is where my mother likes to have her morning prayers," he told me. Her husband had been a Baptist minister.

After the Kerns left on their trip, Grandma Kern took me for a walk on the nearby golf course and we shared stories about our lives. What a never-to-forget week! No cleaning, no cooking. I didn't feel as though I was taking care of Mr. Kern's mother, but rather that *she* was taking care of *me*! I quickly learned that the Kerns were not ostentatious individuals, but very humble, God-centered people.

When the week was over, Grandma Kern gave me a big hug and asked, "You will come and see me again, won't you?"

No Other Choice

Ken Steel was a physics teacher at a high school in Milwaukee, and it was somewhat out of his way to drive me to the college campus every day, so I tacked a note on a student board asking for a ride. The lady placing a note next to mine needed a babysitter. We agreed to exchange babysitting for rides.

We clicked and quickly became good friends. She was Kathy Hawley, the secretary to the head of the chemistry department.

Kathy had always wanted to be a doctor too. She was tenacious and was eventually admitted to medical school, despite her age. She credited her tenacity to watching me. At one point she said, "If you can do it with so little, what's my excuse?"

The demands of caring for her children eventually forced her into pharmacy school, where the hours were less grueling.

It wouldn't be the last time I crossed paths with Kathy.

A Devastating Letter

I was really excited about finishing my thesis and the possibility of entering the medical school at Ohio State to pursue an MD. What really buoyed my hopes was that there was talk of an amnesty program in the U.S. that would provide an opportunity for me to apply for citizenship.

Then I received a devastating letter from the OSU College of Medicine that included this paragraph: "We regret to inform you that the department of Preventive Medicine and Public Health has been downsized. As a result, continuation into the doctoral program has been temporarily suspended. So make your plans accordingly."

I returned to Wisconsin, to my part-time job at the bakery. I also volunteered at the church, answering the phones, cleaning the pews, and doing whatever needed to be done.

It wasn't planned, but I began having discussions about religion with the pastor, Jim Dick. It was at this time I could unabashedly ask all the questions I wanted to—especially concerning doubts I had about God.

I had always believed that if I was faithful to God and did my part, He would be faithful to me, and everything would turn out for the best. But when the pastor's wife died from breast cancer despite all our prayers, my whole belief system seemed to be on a precarious perch. For the first time, I was confronted with the fact that regardless of my wishes, God has a will of His own. Perhaps He didn't just fill orders and requests. Perhaps bad things *do* happen to good people.

As I applied this to my own life, I saw there was the good and the bad, the ups and downs. Yet through it all, the Lord was saying, "Do you trust Me?" In the dark of night, the seeds of doubt tried to take root. In the morning, however, I felt secure in God's love. Life was simple then.

Fly to Freetown?

Two months flew by, then three, then four. At the time I had a student F1 visa, but the medical programs I was interested in required U.S. citizenship.

Deep inside I knew something was going to come through—it was just a matter of time. My objective was to remain in America until that miracle happened.

One day, a story in the newspaper captured my attention. It was about a round trip charter flight from Milwaukee to Paris, France, for two hundred dollars. This seemed quite a bargain. So I researched how much extra it would cost to fly from France to Freetown, Sierra Leone.

BEHIND THE SCENES 79

I jumped at the chance. I could use the thousand dollars I still had sitting in the bank from my OSU windfall to fly to Freetown, collect the data for my master's thesis, and see my family. I shared my plans with the Steeles, and promised I would return. They were very supportive.

In Freetown, what a joy it was to see everyone, especially my grandmother. It was wonderful to connect with childhood friends after several years. The time in Freetown flew by quickly.

The mosquitos were fierce and bold. In fact, the bedroom walls had become a mosaic of patterns left by the smeared blood of long-dead mosquitos that had been swatted on them.

My old books, report cards, and love letters were in a pile and had become part confetti. These were what remained of my childhood records that the mice had chewed away. I was glad I had left my prized *Webster's Dictionary* back in Wisconsin.

The floor boards were now so checkered with holes made by the mice that I could see directly into my grandmother's bedroom from upstairs. I didn't need to run downstairs to ask her anything; I could just speak into one of the holes—no intercom or walkie-talkie needed.

As part of my research project, I spent each day at the offices of Registration of Births and Deaths, a subsection of the Ministry of Health, where I poured over records of deaths due to malnutrition, pneumonia, malaria, and other tropical diseases.

I was startled, however, to find piles of records with the cause of death listed as "Fracture of the 2nd Cervical Vertebrae."

Curious, I asked one day and found out what that meant. After a pronounced silence, someone said, "Broken neck."

"I know that," I quipped. "But how can so many people break their necks?"

There was silence.

The next day, one of the office workers took me aside and said, "You are not in America anymore. When you ask questions like that, you put us all in trouble." He then quietly explained that these were political prisoners who had been hanged.

A few days later I looked into the shoebox where I kept my return plane ticket tucked in with the shoes I had worn on the plane from the States. The edges were now chewed and another pile of confetti of mice droppings lay on the bottom of the box. I took my return plane ticket and placed it in my bra. It remained there until I flew back.

I didn't need to be reminded that I wasn't in America anymore!

My thesis centered on *preventive* medicine versus *curative* medicine as practiced in Sierra Leone, which was approved by OSU when I returned to the States.

Every January in the U.S., to keep my student visa in good standing, I had to register with the Immigration and Naturalization Service (INS). But I had to be a *student!* This now posed a problem: my student visa would soon expire!

A Surprising Interview

Nine months passed. Friends were now asking, "What's your plan?" to which I replied, "Nothing has changed. I am still going to be a doctor; I'm just taking the scenic route to get there." I didn't bother to explain that I had applied to the Department of Microbiology at Michigan State University. Knowledge in immunology and microbiology surely couldn't hurt a medical career. Only a few people at church knew that I had to extend my student visa first.

Without expecting it, I received another call out of the blue. Doris Steele handed me the receiver and it was Bob Kern—the man who had earlier asked me to take care of his mother for a week.

"I know you have been answering phones at the church and making yourself useful, but, Glena, I believe you have so much potential," he said.

What he said next absolutely stunned me. "I made a call to Michigan State University. I have arranged an appointment with the Dean of the College of Medicine. Are you free to fly with me to East Lansing, Michigan, tomorrow?" He added, "We'll see what they have to offer."

I had heard that Bob Kern had connections, but this was above and beyond my wildest dreams. Mr. Kern was the president of Generac, one of the world's largest manufacturers of power generators.

Even more amazing, our conversation with the dean wasn't centered on academics. The two men began talking about church organs, since they were both interested in music. It was almost as if I were being presented as Bob Kern's daughter, especially when he said, "We take care of our children."

The dean then turned to me. "Glena, you are more than welcome to join our program. I want you to go over and talk with Dr. Patterson; she is the director of the Department of Microbiology and will work out your course schedule."

It was all becoming clear. Michigan State already *had* my academic records and knew all about my studies. Bob Kern, with no fanfare or applause, had been silently working behind the scene on my behalf.

Before our meeting with the dean came to a conclusion, he offered, "Glena, you won't be without a church home while you are here. My wife and I will pick you up every Sunday and take you with us to our

Baptist church." To top it off, they invited me to dinner each week after the service. I felt so accepted that I joined the choir.

God's favor was just beginning. I remember thinking, *I don't know why I doubted God. Here He was, at the helm all along.*

Before my first classes, I was in the college bookstore, loading my cart with textbooks. When I reached the cash register, on hearing my name, the woman in charge started rifling through some paperwork. Then she told me, "Please go on through. There seems to be some notes here. We will have to sort it out later. Next!"

I made several stops at the business office to pay for my books, but each time the answer was the same: "We are sorting things out."

Woven into a Tapestry

During my Christmas break, back in Wisconsin at the Steele's home, I told Doris what had occurred—not just at the bookstore, but at the college cafeteria, and with other academic expenses I faced.

She smiled, as if she knew something I didn't.

I have no idea exactly when or why it happened, but the entire First Baptist congregation, including the Kerns obviously decided that I would be their personal project.

When I became a member of First Baptist Church in Waukesha, the theme for that year was "Community." I found out first-hand that this was not just an idle word. They didn't just talk the talk—they walked the walk. I was a living testimony of what a church community does when they become the hands of God extended.

There were many angels woven into the tapestry of my life without my knowledge, without my solicitation.

Where would these miracles lead?

CHAPTER TEN

A TORN LETTER

Saturday nights were special at Michigan State. That's when a group of international students would each chip in two dollars and together prepare a traditional recipe from a particular country. One week it was Pho Ga from Vietnam; the next it could be Seafood Paella from Spain or Bangladeshi Beef Curry. It was a culinary adventure!

The group was an eclectic mix of men and women enrolled in master's programs but some, who were U.S. citizens, were already working on their MD.

Here I was, taking advance classes in microbiology, yet seeing no path to enter an MD program in America.

One night, I overheard a classmate talking about a new medical school in Africa, and my ears perked up. He said, "The Vatican, the United States, and the United Nations are working on a project to educate Africans—in Africa."

The next day I began investigating and learned of the Mano River Union project.

The Mano river originates in Guinea and flows to form part of the Sierra Leone-Liberia border. In 1973 the Mano River Union was created. Its announcement of plans to build the John F. Kennedy

Hospital in Monrovia, Liberia, and the training of future doctors from Guinea, Sierra Leone, and Liberia was well underway.

My mental wheels went into overdrive: *If I can't get into medical school in America, why not go to Liberia?* So I applied.

The Telegram

Several weeks went by with no response from Africa.

And then, near the end of my program in Lansing, as I was preparing a talk I had been asked to give on Legionaires' disease, things finally began to happen.

I remember that Tuesday afternoon well. A girl from my dorm came running up, waving something in her hand. "I have some mail for you," she exclaimed.

The envelope was ripped in half, but my name was written on the outside. When I pulled out what was left of the enclosed letter, it was a mangled mess.

I could only decipher two or three sentences. One read, "You will be required to make an advance deposit for use of a lab microscope." Another part detailed, "You will need the following books," but I couldn't find the list. However, I could make out the words, "Please contact the director of Library Services." Down at the bottom of the letter were the words "The Medical College of Liberia."

Wondering what it meant, I sent a telegram to the Medical College in Monrovia explaining the situation. "Whatever correspondence you recently sent me was damaged in transit, and I only received a portion of it. Would you please resend the letter?" Two days later there was a returned telegram saying, "You have been accepted into our program. You must be here to register by (such and such a date)."

I went to the Registrar's Office and quickly withdrew my status as a student of Michigan State University.

The Yellow Banana

The words *excited* and *exhilarated* don't begin to express how I felt. My emotions were registering 12 on a 10-point scale. I ran back to my room and called the Steeles, who rejoiced with me. They phoned practically everybody in the church, including the Kerns, to relate the good news.

Bob Kern sent a driver to Lansing to pick up me and my "stuff" for the trip back to Wisconsin. I'll never forget the car. It was a Toyota with a raised trunk that looked like a "Yellow Banana," which is exactly what the driver called it.

I turned in my dorm key and said good-bye to Michigan. Seated in the Yellow Banana, the imagery of the driver in the front at the wheel with me in the back wasn't lost on me. I imagined God at the wheel, taking me to my longed-for destination.

Back in Waukesha, with a few weeks to spare before leaving, I returned to my part time job at the bakery.

A Night for Glena

My friends at First Baptist Church were more than kind. In fact, they set aside a special night and asked me to share my story.

With a grateful heart, I thanked them for the love and support they had showered on an unknown foreign student. "I am now going to complete the work God has called me to do," I told the congregation.

The church presented me with the classic *Stedman's Medical Dictionary*, with over 50,000 entries and more than a thousand illustrations. Inscribed on the first page were these words:

Glena, thank you for allowing us to witness Christ's commission in action through you. Our thoughts and prayers are with you as you continue your education and go into your life's work. This dictionary represents only a part of what you have done for us.

It was dated March 20, 1977. If my heart was full that night, my head was even fuller. Full of ideas so grandiose, so naive, that even I smiled. *Coming home on the S.S Apapa to a hero's welcome. "Glena finds cure for malaria,"* a banner would read. It was my dream. I could dream as much as I wanted.

A reporter from the *Waukesha Freeman* was present, and the next day the paper printed a big article highlighting an African girl who had been embraced by the First Baptist community. It detailed how she had been accepted into medical school in Liberia and was returning to the continent of her birth. There was also a photo of me surrounded by my church family.

"Does This Girl Look Familiar?"

The following morning, I rode my bike from the Steele's house to the bakery. To my surprise, the owner called me into his office—something he had never done before since I had very little contact with him.

He was holding the local newspaper and told me, "I've been reading the most heartwarming story."

"What's it about?" I asked.

"There's a girl from Africa who is going back to her people and is studying to be a doctor. A local church has really taken her under their wing and showed her great kindness." Then he added, "There's no telling what a person can do if they put their mind to it."

Innocently, I asked, "Can I see the article?"

When he handed it to me, I held the photo in front of his face and asked, "Does this girl look familiar?"

Before he could answer, I said, "That's me."

At first he probably thought I was teasing, but when the reality of the moment hit him, his face turned bright red.

I probably should have let that be the end of the story, but thinking about what had happened in the past, I couldn't help myself. I continued, "The first day I came here, I walked into this bakery looking for a job. You graciously offered me one but didn't ask me to sign my name on the employment form, but rather just place an 'X' on the signature line. You automatically assumed I was illiterate."

By now the boss was way beyond embarrassed. My intent was not to humiliate him, but to let him know that you can't always judge a book by its cover and snap judgments are often wrong. I never saw him again, but I believe it was a life lesson that neither of us would ever forget.

What Was God's Blueprint?

I guess you could call me naive, but so many things had fallen into place in America that I knew somehow the Lord would take care of my future. I had no inkling of how I would pay for my plane fare from Chicago to West Africa, but again, without asking, it was taken care of.

On the long flight I began to mull over questions that millions of others before me had pondered. *Why was I placed on this earth? What am I supposed to accomplish?*

I realized that I didn't choose to come into this world; it was the doing of a higher power. But now that I was here, it was becoming obvious that God was equipping me with the tools to fulfill His purpose and complete what He intended for me to do. I concluded, "I may have some hurdles to jump, but God is in control. Everything I have comes from His hand."

It is for this reason that I believe, as someone once wrote, "God, in His wisdom and love, very often sends His angels down to walk with us. . . . We know them best as 'friends.'" Every friend in my life was placed there by my heavenly Father's design. Each opportunity was a door opened from above.

I also thought about receiving the telegram of acceptance from the Medical School in Liberia. To me, it was a no-brainer, because I firmly believed it was part of God's divine plan for Glena. I must admit, however, that it took a long time to bring me to the point of boarding that plane.

I had no idea of the challenges waiting for me on the other side of the Atlantic Ocean. I once again was willing and ready to navigate that sea with my face turned east toward Africa. I sensed the spirit of my ancestors. I felt the same trepidation when they too had faced this identical ocean and returned to Africa. They had hope, as did I.

I had steered through the twists and turns of academic life and survived—and I knew without a shadow of doubt that God had a blueprint for my future.

CHAPTER ELEVEN

THE MAN OF MY DREAMS?

To my relief, the ten-hour nonstop flight to Monrovia was practically empty, so I had a complete row to myself and could settle down in comfort. A couple of hours into the journey, a very friendly woman walked over to where I was seated and introduced herself. "Hi, my name is Ellen. What part of Africa are you headed for?" she asked.

"I'm going to Monrovia to enroll in medical school," I replied. We then entered into a long conversation about medicine, economics, American culture, and several other topics. I was impressed with her breadth of knowledge on practically any topic.

It was late at night when we arrived at the airport. The Medical College had written to say they would have someone there to meet me. After claiming my luggage, I went to the information desk and was told they would be closing the airport in a few minutes. About that time, a young man arrived and told me he was the driver for Ellen, the woman I had met on the airplane. She was already seated in her car, but she beckoned me over.

She suggested, "Since no one is here to meet you, why don't you come and stay at my house tonight, and we'll sort everything out in the morning."

What I didn't know, but soon found out, my new friend was

Ellen Johnson Sirleaf, who at the time was the Minister of Finance for the country of Liberia—and who later became the president of the nation in 2006.

My angels are always with me.

The next morning, her driver took me to the Medical College, where an administrator deeply apologized for the mixup at the airport, gave me some paperwork to fill out, and told me, "Classes start in two weeks."

Ellen once again came to my rescue. For the next fourteen days, she treated me like a member of her family, and we enjoyed thought-provoking discussions that would last late into the night.

A Tap on My Shoulder

The new Medical College was truly a model of cooperation. The Vatican had birthed the idea, the United States had supplied most of the finances, and Liberia provided the manpower for construction. The Medical School was a mini-United Nations. Although the project was construed to educate doctors for West Africa, applicants came from all over Africa, including Nigeria, South Africa, Angola, Tanzania, Zimbabwe, and Lesotho—plus international students from nations such as India, Sri Lanka, and the United States. The professors, too, were from all over the world: Romania, Australia, Sierra Leone, Rwanda, USA, Egypt, Japan, Norway.

It was a seven-year program. Five years of medical training, one year of compulsory internship, and one year of rural service in Liberia.

One day I was snapping pictures of the JFK Hospital with my instamatic camera to send back to Wisconsin when a young man tapped me on my shoulder and commented, "Pictures are much

THE MAN OF MY DREAMS? 91

more meaningful when a person is in them." So now it was *me* in the photos.

A couple of days later, I was at the office of the program administration, a few blocks from the hospital, and I saw a bus with the words "Medical College" posted on the front. "Where does that bus go?" I asked a man in charge.

He replied, "The girls don't live on campus, so this bus transports them to their classes, during lunch breaks, and back to their dorms in the evening. Other students can also use it, and it's free."

"Can I take a trial ride?" I asked.

"Sure," the man said, "Hop on board."

As I walked toward the back of the bus, I passed the same young man who had taken my picture on campus. And the next thing I knew, he rose from his seat, walked back, and sat down right beside me. Trying not to look too interested, I couldn't help but notice that he was well-dressed, his shoes were shined, and he was dapper like my brother.

I learned that his name was Kylkon Makwi, and he was from a village near Gbarnga, about a hundred miles northeast of Monrovia. During our short conversation, he told me he had spent some time in the US, which explained his slight American accent. I felt a kinship with him.

I don't know if it was coincidence or calculation, but I kept bumping into this guy practically every day.

Late one afternoon, he knocked on the door of my dorm room. "Sorry to bother you," he began. "It's my roommate's birthday today, and I bought two tickets to the movies tonight. I think he made plans with his family, and I was wondering if you would like to see the film with me."

"What time?" I asked.

"Seven o'clock," he replied.

"Oh, I'll never make it by then!" I answered.

"Well, how about the nine o'clock showing?" he suggested.

I agreed to go with him, thinking, *What a smooth operator. He didn't really buy two tickets for seven o'clock.* Movie tickets in Monrovia are theatre- and time-specific. If you bought a ticket for a seven o'clock show, you could not use it for a nine o'clock showing. I had an inkling he was putting me on.

The Competition

Kylkon and I began dating, but I constantly told him, "Don't you think you are spending too much time with me? You should be studying." He didn't seem to get the message.

It was 1978. I found the men in Liberia just as chauvinistic as some I had met in America. On campus there were plenty of international students, but most of them were men, because medicine at that time in Africa was mostly a masculine discipline.

Before class one morning, I overheard one of my classmates telling a friend, "This program takes seven years, and some women think they are going to beat me to the finish line—but they have another thing coming!"

Although he wasn't talking directly to me, I got the gist of what he was saying. From then on I made it my personal goal to beat him at everything.

When month-end test results were released, they were posted only as the median and the range. This was meant as a guide to inform you how you stood with the rest of the class. One particular day, I saw that the median was 78 and the range was from 45 to 92. I looked at my score, which was the high number. So I decided to play a game with my arrogant classmate.

THE MAN OF MY DREAMS?

"I see you got a 92. How did you manage that?" I asked him.

He replied, beaming proudly, "No, I got a 91."

"Show me," I said.

When he did, I pulled out my 92.

We played this game until graduation. Silently I enjoyed deflating his ego, but it also helped me remain focused.

An incident at MSU emboldened me to play this game. I recall feeling intimidated by the mere presence of a large number of medical students who had signed up for the microbiology lab session I was registered in. Then Charles, one of the medical students, loudly refused to have me as his lab partner, despite the encouragement of the instructor. He chose instead to pair with two other med students, leaving me with no partner.

The lab instructor was a rather bellicose woman, and her first words did not allay any of my fears. I certainly didn't feel I belonged there. She announced, "A good number of you will not pass this course. However, I will give you advanced notice of your standing well before your final grade. At some point I will list on the blackboard only the names of the people who are in trouble."

It was several weeks later that, upon entering the lab, she turned her back to the class and made two columns on the board.

My humiliation was complete. In one column was just my name. On the second column were three other names.

She then turned to face the class and said, "If your name is not on the board, you are okay. For those listed in column two, you can ask the person named in column one to help you with the concepts covered between weeks seven and nine. If you do not wish to do so, I suggest you drop the class."

Charles did not wish to ask for my help. He chose to drop the class. I was relieved immensely, and I also gained a bit of stature among the rest of the students.

A Question on the Beach

Kylkon was soft-spoken, handsome, and a good listener. I felt honored that he chose to spend time with me instead of other girls who appeared way more attractive than me.

One day during lunchtime, we took a walk along the beach—the Medical School campus was just a few yards away. He stopped, looked me in the eyes, and, to my surprise, said, "Glena, I want to ask your mother for her daughter's hand in marriage."

Half-joking, I replied, "I don't think my two brothers-in-law would take very kindly to that!"

Kylkon laughed and said, "No, I'm talking about *you!*"

I paused for a moment and then told him, "That's a nice thought, but we must think about what that would mean for both of us." I added, "My number one goal is not marriage; it's to become a physician. That is my calling. But if we do get married, I will not have any children until I have my degree."

I ended by saying, "If all these conditions are okay with you, I am certainly open to marriage."

To be honest, I had such tunnel vision regarding my goal that not even marriage interested me. What I didn't understand, however, was that most of the medical students didn't approve of our relationship. In not-so-subtle ways they seemed to imply, "He's too good-looking for you" or "He should be marrying a Liberian girl."

My mother, in her wildest dreams, never thought I wanted to get married since I had become so hostile to men because of the way my father had treated her. I was leery of a man's motives and thought:

THE MAN OF MY DREAMS?

He would leave me with children, and my life would be over. I would be like my mother—absolutely no way!

Finally, during my second year of medical school, I wrote my mom a letter, telling her about the wonderful person I had met and my decision to marry him. Arrangements were made to have the 1979 wedding at the Methodist church in Freetown.

I sent letters to my friends in Wisconsin, and they were as excited as I was. Doris even wrote saying, "Yes, get out of those blue jeans. Put on some earrings and curl your hair." The letter was accompanied by two new dresses she had made me.

Ken and Doris Steele flew over for the big occasion. When they arrived in Monrovia, I told them that we had been invited to meet Kylkon's father in his village. They had no idea what they were in for. After a three-hour drive over rough, bumpy roads to Gbarnga, we set out on foot for our final destination. My future father-in-law's village was a four-hour trek in sweltering heat, through vine-covered paths, with the sounds of wildlife in the canopy above—it was the *real* Africa. We had our mosquito spray and bottles of water, and we kept up our spirits by singing choruses we had learned at church.

When we arrived at the small village, Kylkon's father was not there, but we spent time with his sister, a lovely person who welcomed us warmly.

After everything the Steeles had done for me, it was my joy to show them parts of Sierra Leone before they flew back to Wisconsin.

A Startling Suggestion

My new husband and I settled into married life in Monrovia.

Kylkon was one year ahead of me at the Medical College; I was in preclinical, and he was just starting his clinicals.

At the end of the school year, I was genuinely happy. Not only did I have a gold ring adorning my finger, but I had stellar grades. I wore the biggest smile on my face, but the other students looked at me as if to say, "What is she so upbeat about?"

I was healthy, married, making good grades, and my life was secure. I didn't ask Kylkon about his grades, because I assumed he was doing just fine. I would continue to chat with God, pointing out that as per our arrangement, if He would help me, I would do my best. I certainly thought I was doing just that.

Then, two weeks before classes were to start again, my husband made a startling suggestion. He said, "You have a master's degree from the States, so why don't you get a job at the Ministry of Health?"

"Why would I want to do that?" I responded, quite puzzled.

"Because I think it's time we start a family," he told me, half-demanding. "Think it over, and we can talk about it tomorrow."

The next day, he pressed, "So what's your decision?"

"I thought we had settled this issue before I agreed to marry you," I responded. "Children would just complicate our lives, and besides, who's going to take care of them? And how am I going to live with myself if I leave everything I've been preparing for? No, that's not what I want to do."

Then he dropped a bombshell: "Well, I am going to be your classmate."

"What are you saying?"

"I didn't pass the requirements, and it looks like I will have to repeat the entire year," he shamefully admitted.

It was what it was—and I knew we'd have to adjust to reality.

Just Gossip?

I really didn't think much about it when Kylkon started arriving home later and later each night. Most of the expatriate professors left campus around six or seven o'clock in the evening, but he would get home around nine. At first, I thought, *He's just working late in the clinic or studying in the auditorium to improve his grades.*

But then late one night I had finished my duties and was walking back from the hospital to our apartment. In the distance I saw the profile of a man who looked just like Kylkon. *Surely that couldn't be him,* I thought. But when I reached home, he wasn't there.

Again, I tried to dismiss any negative thoughts from my mind.

Things reached a boiling point, though, when a classmate came up to me and casually said, "I think Kylkon is in big trouble."

"Why would you say such a thing?" I demanded.

"He pushed a woman down a flight of steps in her dorm," she continued.

"Who was it?" I questioned.

As if I already knew the answer, she blurted out, "Oh, it was his girlfriend."

Girlfriend? *Girlfriend?*

At that moment, I realized that everyone on campus knew more about my husband than I did—the one who was happy with her life and oblivious to his failures. Evidently I was the only person who *didn't* know about his lady friend.

Filled with shame, I stifled my feelings in front of my husband. Instead of blowing up, my mind was whirling, wondering how my marriage could be saved. If I started to bring up the issue, he would quickly shut me down, saying, "Oh, you've been listening to far too much gossip."

When I was alone, my tears would not stop flowing. Was history repeating itself in *my* life?

More Than Anger

I had developed a strong friendship with my anatomy professor, Dr. Lazar from Romania. Brushing aside my shame, I went to his office. On seeing me, he asked, "All you all right?" Then he noted that he had seen me fall asleep in class more than once over the last few days. He also questioned me about the bruises he noticed on my arms and face.

Through my tears, I confided in him. "Things are not as they seem." Then I related all that had taken place regarding my husband.

Dr. Lazar was sympathetic and supportive. He made me promise to keep studying. "And if he is hitting you, you must leave him," he told me firmly.

Inside I was more than angry. *What had I done to deserve this? Didn't I keep my marriage vows?*

Things went from bad to worse. On my way to the first of three days of exams, I saw Kylkon embrace a woman under a tree. They both looked straight at me as my world fell apart before my eyes. I was emotionless. I couldn't scream. I couldn't cry. I was totally numb.

Pulling myself together, I reminded myself, *Glena, you know how to compartmentalize. Go to the auditorium and finish what you set out to do.*

I repeated this for the three testing days—and then totally collapsed in exhaustion, both mentally and physically.

A few months later a woman with a baby cradled in her arms knocked on our door looking for Kylkon. I presumed he had some medical records that she needed. When I explained he wasn't home, she waited outside for a long time before leaving.

When I later learned that Kylkon was the baby's father, I actually vomited.

I was so immersed in my studies and so in love with my husband that I had blinders on. I tried to make excuses for all his behavior; I'd had too many detours. I wanted calm, peace, and love.

What had happened to my perfect dream that there would be only one man in my life with whom I would grow old with? Was my bus careening off track? Or had I stepped off the bus entirely? I felt very alone.

You can presume that someone looks intelligent until they speak and prove you wrong. Likewise, you can think you see kindness in a person's eyes. But it isn't what you look at—it's what you see! Kylkon was neither wise nor kind. I could see that now.

Earlier, my blinders were on too tightly.

CHAPTER TWELVE

WHAT MORE COULD GO WRONG?

My days became increasingly stressful, but I did my best to hide the tension bubbling under the surface. Kylkon had filed divorce papers with the court, but in Liberia the process can go on forever.

We were separated, yet we were not apart. Both of us were in our third year of medical school, which meant we shared several classes together. I would see him almost every day.

Even more, I was very embarrassed about the possibility of divorce that I didn't say a word to my mother, or mention it in my letters to my friends back in Wisconsin. I was hoping beyond hope that somehow we could reconcile.

I tried making concessions. Kylkon still had the key to our apartment, and I let him drop off his clothes that needed washing. At home, things were less tense. I could make him laugh; when we laughed, I felt better. In class, however, he would find some way to humiliate me. Each day, before the instructor arrived, he would drop a wadded note on my desk, and walk to his seat. When I opened the scrunched up paper, it would read, "Your hair looks like a rat's nest." He knew how to push my buttons because he knew how much I hated my hair. The high humidity wreaked havoc with it.

After a few weeks of this harassment, out of frustration and anger I started retaliating out loud—much to the amusement of the rest of the students who thought it was hilarious. It became class entertainment, and before long it became a campus soap opera.

I felt alone and ashamed.

It reached the point where I could no longer bear to open the notes, and one day, overcome as to how low our relationship had sunk, I walked out into the hallway and began to bawl like a baby. I soon realized that I too was part of the problem. I resolved to not touch the notes and either leave them on my desk or throw them on the floor.

I was unaware that about this time, the dean of the Medical College and several professors had called a confidential meeting to discuss what they had perceived to be a problem between Kylkon and me. One supervisor evidently said, "His academics are sliding and her emotions are suffering—and we may lose them both."

Kylkon always appeared calm, but this was a tumultuous time for me. My preclinical days were ending.

Since I socialized with no one, it made me seem aloof. I spent all day on campus, ate my lunch on the beach alone, and spent long nights in the hospital auditorium studying. I only had to cross the street to get to my apartment, where I would nap, shower, and get ready for the next day.

I kept my tongue sharp and barbed, ready with a quick response. I was tired of the constant references made to me about the whereabouts of my husband.

In our small class of sixteen students, I took secret pleasure in beating my male colleagues in academics. I know I seemed arrogant.

When our class started clinical rotations, my long nights were now spent in the hospital. When I started my obstetrics rotation, I spent most of my nights at the maternity center. There was no one at home.

The obstetrics professor seemed to be encouraging me to pursue a career in that specialty. He was especially impressed with my log book. While we were encouraged to participate in at least one hundred normal deliveries, I had well over six hundred entries, all witnessed and signed by the supervising doctors. The high pregnancy rate made this easy to accomplish.

At the end of the semester I was quite dismayed to see that I received a C- in obstetrics. I had passed all the final exams with scores in the high 90s. There had to be a mistake.

I later learned that I had offended him. One of the premed students once stopped me on campus to say the obstetric professor's boots, which he wore to the operating room, were missing. Being ever present at the maternity center, he wondered if I knew where they were. Without thinking, I replied that perhaps he should look for them where he last slept.

I often would forget my rain boots by the auditorium doors or by a classroom door during the rainy season. But when the student relayed my answer back to him, the professor thought I was implying that he was promiscuous. I didn't get a chance to explain, as I had started another clinical rotation by then.

The following year I sent word to him that the C- minus grade was punitive. I also let him know I was aware that he had remarked, "That girl needs to be brought down a notch." Instead of making an appointment with him to explain and apologize, I simply shot a note back, "I thought grades were *earned,* not *awarded.*"

I was well on my way to earning my "pugilistic bitch" stripes!

Home for Christmas?

The day I had been crying in the hallway, I was approached by one of the pharmacology professors. "What's wrong?" he asked, seeing my distress.

"What's *not* wrong?" I answered. He seemed sympathetic, but since I didn't know him, I was hesitant to share any details.

Later that semester, I bumped into Dr. Mac again—everyone called him that. He was a peculiar looking man with red hair. That week he was sporting a Salvador Dali-type mustache.

I had heard that his classes were enjoyable and that he used great analogies to get his points across. "Are you going to teach us next year?" I asked him one day as we crossed paths in the hallway.

The six-foot-two professor looked down on me and replied, "Only if you pass!" Then he smiled.

For whatever reason, he took an interest in both me and Kylkon. As December approached, he asked me, "Is Kylkon coming home for Christmas?"

Kylkon had been up-country doing some special field work. The college administration thought he might do better academically if he was away from marital discord.

Dr. Mac continued, "Everybody comes home for Christmas, so why don't you make some preparations?" I had the distinct impression he had talked with Kylkon.

A few days later, Dr. Mac called me to his office and asked, "What plans are you making to return to the U.S. and transfer to a medical school there?"

"Why would I do that?" I answered, dumbfounded.

"Well," he continued, "Your husband has asked me to write a letter of recommendation to Loma Linda Hospital in Southern California. He wants to transfer there."

To which I responded, "I am making no such plans."

Dr. Mac took it upon himself to befriend Kylkon, and over a beer he told him, "You don't appreciate what you have in Glena. You agreed to enter into a marriage, and even though you made some bad choices, she didn't abandon or bad-mouth you. She is continuing on her chosen path, so can't you meet her halfway? I am sure she will forgive you."

The day before Christmas arrived. In the afternoon I cooked a special chicken dish for the next day, and that Christmas Eve went to a late night candlelight service at a local church. Later, as I was walking to my apartment, Dr. Mac's car pulled up. He rolled down his window and inquired, "Is he here yet?"

He seemed genuinely disappointed when I answered, "No." Then I added, "I hope you, your wife, and children have a wonderful Christmas."

"Thanks," he responded, "but we don't have any children." I didn't know much about his personal life, but I couldn't help wondering, *Why does he care about us?*

I spent Christmas alone, ashamed and devastated that my marriage had reached this point, yet lying to myself and still holding on to a thread of hope.

See, I said to myself, *if Dr. Mac thinks this can be worked out, my bus couldn't be so off track after all . . .* But my heart sank like a stone.

Peeling a Tangerine

It was announced that all medical students were to attend a conference at a Lutheran medical center located about 112 miles from JFK Hospital. The bus would leave the dorm area at 7:00 a.m. Since I would be finishing an all-night rotation, I asked the students to have the driver pick me up at the hospital.

It was 9:00 a.m. and I was still standing outside in my white coat, patiently waiting. The chief of surgery came out and asked, "Are you going to the conference?"

After I explained that the bus failed to pick me up, he told me, "I'm on my way to the same conference. Would you like a ride?"

I knew who the chief of surgery was, but not having done a surgical rotation yet, I had never spoken to him.

About halfway to our destination, we stopped at a roadside stand to purchase some mangos, peanuts, and a couple of tangerines.

After we had run out of medical topics to discuss, he turned to me and asked, "So, what's the latest gossip on campus?"

I explained, "I don't live on campus."

So he continued, "Let me tell you what's happening with the Makwis."

At the time, I was peeling a tangerine, and I froze in my seat. *"No,* I thought, *"not this soap opera nonsense again."*

He started rattling off a bunch of half-truths. "Mrs. Makwi really takes advantage of her husband; he seems so calm and docile."

"Yes," I interjected, "I have seen him."

He continued, "She curses him in class. They have relatives in America who send them money for an apartment, but she has kicked him out."

I could feel my heart racing, but I decided to play along and asked, "What was so bad about the woman if he wanted to marry her in the first place?"

He backtracked a little, saying, "Well, she is known to be funny, very bright, and is an excellent student."

For the remainder of the journey, I let him tell his soap opera story, interrupting only to egg him on for more.

When I could clearly see the entrance to the hospital, I turned to him and in the strongest voice I could muster, I said, "Sir, I am Mrs. Makwi."

"Oh, I am so sorry," he stammered, apologizing profusely.

"That's okay," I responded. "But I want you to know that what you've heard could not be further from the truth."

I was appalled and baffled that a man of his education and stature would listen to such garbage, let alone repeat it. With my voice shaking, I told him, "I have never wronged my husband, but you need to know that he is a cheater and a deceiver. I too was fooled by his calm demeanor. The only contract that I have is between me and my God, and everything else will fall by the wayside."

When the car finally stopped, I was still trembling, but I managed to mumble, "Thanks for the ride."

I don't think I learned anything at the conference that day. Months later, during my surgical rotation, I ran into the chief of surgery several times. I likely did not endear myself to him—perhaps it was that smirk on my face.

The Coup

In the spring of 1980, on April 12 to be exact, all hell broke loose. Not between me and Kylkon, but in the nation of Liberia.

Early that morning, a rebel group of noncommissioned officers and an indigenous faction of the Armed Forces of Liberia under the command of Master Sargent Samuel Doe stormed the presidential palace in Monrovia and overthrew president William Tolbert Jr. It was a violent coup.

Their grievance was the fact that since Liberia's independence in 1847, the leadership of the country held close ties to the United

States, and the rebels wanted that relationship to end. Tolbert's body, together with twenty-seven other victims, was dumped into a mass grave, with a crowd of angry Liberians shouting insults and throwing rocks at the corpses.

Within the next two weeks, most of the cabinet members of the Tolbert administration had been put on trial in a kangaroo court and sentenced to death. Many of them were publicly executed at a beach near the Barclay Training Center in Monrovia.

Only four members of the Tolbert administration survived the takeover and its aftermath; among them was the Minister of Finance, future President Ellen Johnson Sirleaf—the woman who gave me a ride to her home the night I first arrived in Liberia.

A Conflicted Graduation

"Glena, you need to keep a low profile and watch your step."

That was the advice I received at the hospital—especially since I had American ties. My closest friends were missionary expatriates at the Lutheran church compound.

Soldiers were patrolling the streets, and military trucks were speeding by—no other vehicles were allowed on the road. For a while classes at the Medical School were suspended because students couldn't make it to the hospital. The country was running on rumors.

During this time, I was walking near the American Embassy and saw Dr. Mac standing on a balcony, waving at me. He invited me over to meet his wife and talk about the dangerous situation in Monrovia. It would be more than a year before I saw him again.

Meanwhile, the animosity between my husband and me had died down since we were no longer taking classes together. His application to the courts for a divorce still remained in limbo.

At the end of my fifth year of medical school, it was finally graduation day. None of my family members were able to attend.

As I looked into the crowded stands, I was momentarily overcome with sadness. I wished my mother had been with me that day. This medical degree was a fitting retribution for the degradation my father had heaped on her that ugly night so long ago. Maybe there was some other way I could make it up to her.

Ahead was a year of internship at JFK hospital, followed by a year of national service in one of the counties away from Monrovia.

It was with mixed emotions that I read the name on my diploma: Glena Davies Makwi.

CHAPTER THIRTEEN

A PLACE CALLED ZORZOR

My face breaks into a smile when I think about the graduating ceremony at the medical school in Liberia. Our class was lined up according to rank. I was the only class member with a master's degree; everyone else had a bachelor's degree. They placed me at the back of the line.

There I was, proudly dressed in a borrowed cap and gown. When I received my diploma, the entire audience burst into applause—not because they knew me, but because I was a woman. Oh, well!

One of the benefits of being in the top tier of my graduating class was an all expense-paid three-month internship at any medical school in America that would accept me. I was accepted at the University of Michigan, Ann Arbor. It was close enough to Wisconsin to allow me to visit my friends.

There was only one problem, however. I didn't have the proper documentation for an exit visa. According to Liberian rules at the time, I needed a father, a husband, or an adult male son to vouch for me.

There had been no official action on my divorce proceedings, and Makwi was the name written on my diploma. In desperation, I went to the Dean of Women and pleaded for her help. Thankfully, she found the paperwork of my original application to medical school and attached it to a document that stated I truly was Glena Davies. Fortunately this satisfied the customs authorities.

The Steeles arranged for me to stay with the family of an Anglican minister in Lansing for my short "externship." Then, during a two-week break before returning to Africa, I visited Pewaukee, Genesee, and Waukesha. During this time I realized that the tiny tendrils that had sprouted while I had lived in Wisconsin had now grown into roots.

Thinking Ahead

The remainder of my one-year internship was spent at the JFK Hospital in Monrovia. Life was good. Internship came with an apartment and a monthly stipend.

I wrote to the church in Wisconsin, thanking them for their kindness over the years, and I let them know they no longer needed to send me funds, as I was now on my own and self-sufficient.

By Christmas of that year I had saved up nearly two thousand dollars and dreamed of buying a piece of land in Freetown and eventually building a house where my mother could live. Our family home on 38 Waterloo Street had always been a rental—and it was literally falling apart.

About that time, a childhood friend of mine showed up in Monrovia. It was the daughter of Dr. Cole, one of the two girls I used to accompany to school at their father's request. She told me she was engaged, and her fiancé was in Liberia studying to be a doctor.

In the course of our conversation, she mentioned that her dad was trying to raise some money because times were tough in Freetown and he was supporting another daughter attending university in England. She also told me that her father knew of a plot of land that would be perfect for my future plans.

The price was a thousand dollars. There was no signed document, but every time Dr. Cole's daughter or wife came to visit their future son-in-law, I would give them some cash to take back toward the purchase. I told them, "Please don't tell my mother; I want this to be a big surprise."

During that spring, my mind started whirling at the prospect of being a land owner. I even thought about setting up a medical practice in Freetown with a house for me and my mom on the same property.

Then I received word that Dr. Cole had found an even better site, one that cost only a little more. I decided to make a trip to Sierra Leone to see it in person. When I arrived home, my mother was angry and in tears, and she began lashing out at me. "Why didn't you tell me that you were buying some land and planned to live near all those rich people?

"What are you talking about?" I asked, puzzled.

Evidently Dr. Cole had approached my mother and demanded that she give him some money to make an immediate down payment on the better piece of property that she, of course, knew nothing about. My mom had no such financial resources.

It was then I explained to her, "Sisi, this is all for you. I wanted to surprise you with a new house." She wouldn't have to deal with cockroaches, mice and, of course, the much-hated latrine.

It took quite a while for this news to sink in.

On that visit, I gave Dr. Cole the extra two hundred dollars, and he promised that he would arrange all the paperwork. I still had not physically seen the land, but I was in no hurry since I had another half year of internship ahead, plus a year of mandatory rural service.

Finally, Real Medicine

During lunch breaks with fellow interns, the topic often turned to the "stories" people had heard about the terrible conditions at some of the rural hospitals in Liberia—especially the ones that were isolated and almost impossible to reach. The reputation of many of the interior medical facilities was horrible. I'm not sure if any of the stories were true, but I was frightened at the prospect of serving alone in the more remote areas. I made a mental list of the places that, if possible, I would try to avoid.

I decided to make a visit to the Minister of Health, and when I reached the building, I noticed that two of his assistants were helping him into his car—evidently he was having some physical problems. I stopped him for a moment and said, "Sir, I know you are the person who decides where rural service officers are to be assigned."

He interrupted me and asked, "Where would you like to go?"

"Either Zorzor or Ganta." I named a couple of other possibilities I had heard were good too.

"What is your name, child?" he inquired.

When I told him, he asked one of his assistants to write it down. I was elated—especially when I soon learned that I had been assigned to the Curran Lutheran Hospital in Zorzor. It was about 150 miles from Monrovia, reached by paved and dirt roads, on the border of Guinea.

Although the town could not pass as a tourist destination, the people were warm, loving, and inclusive. It consisted of a few hundred mud huts and shanty houses with tin roofs. The hospital, however, was its main claim to fame, founded by missionaries in 1924.

The staff came from America, India, Europe, and many other parts of the world, and the compound also included a nursing school. I was now no longer an intern but a medical officer of the Liberian government, being paid a full salary.

This was my introduction to *real* medicine and practicing

procedures I had never been taught. It was exciting. There was so much to see, do, and learn. Each day brought its own challenges, but when a life was saved, we all rejoiced. Death was always lurking. It claimed many lives, especially those of women and children.

If a young man accidently shot himself when hunting bush meat, we had to amputate the limb. There was no rehab.

Among the women, we didn't see many normal deliveries—the nurses and midwives took care of that since they were experts in this area.

Repairing inguinal hernias was a daily routine. They were found in hardworking men who cut down trees, cleaned brush to create farmland, and lifted very heavy loads to make a living.

For some reason, the cases that came in at night were much more challenging and interesting.

Under the Bandana

I was off duty one evening when the hospital truck pulled up and the driver said, "Dr. Hove needs you immediately."

Of course, I rushed right over. As I walked into the room where he was working, there was a smell I will never forget. It was rotting flesh.

In one corner was a tall woman with a bandana over the bridge of her nose. Her son was standing in the opposite corner. She would reach under the bandana and spit in a cup. Dr. Hove was there, shining a bright light into her mouth.

He turned to me and said, "Glena, I have been here picking these maggots out for four hours and I must have a break. I need to go home. Can you help me?"

When I lifted the bandana, in the roof of her mouth was a hole where the flesh had rotted away. The light revealed the shadows of moving objects. I almost vomited on the spot. This was the worst case of myiasis I would ever encounter.

The woman had been taken to the forest and left there to die. Nobody wanted her; not even the witch doctors could help. It was as if she was being eaten from the inside out.

Her son was a taxi driver who drove all over Liberia. But when he went to visit his mother, he learned she had been taken to the forest. He told me, "I didn't have a chance to say good-bye, so I went looking for her."

He found out that his mother's problem began when she suffered with a toothache, and someone at the village market sold her snuff to pack around the infected tooth to ease the pain. Evidently the snuff was infested with eggs which happily hatched into maggots. They then ate their way through her gums and into her palate.

Now it was my task to finish the job of pulling out the rest of the crawling maggots. This wasn't in any of my medical training manuals!

A few months later, Dr. Hove and I were attending a conference at Phebe Hospital, a few hours away. A woman with a rather deformed face came up to us. She wore a big smile, but had only two teeth. Dr. Hove turned to me and whispered, "Do you remember her? This is the maggot lady!"

The three of us hugged.

The "Kill Me Quick" Journeys

In rural areas of Africa, most of the women gave birth at home, but some walk for days to deliver their baby in the hospital. These were usually women who were having complications. Many of the births resulted in C-sections.

A PLACE CALLED ZORZOR

While I was at Zorzor, I began to uderstand the need for pediatrics. There was a desperate need for mothers to be better educated as to how to keep their children free from diseases and provide them with better nutrition. The seeds for my passion for pediatrics were planted here.

Maternal deaths were unacceptably high, and I became preoccupied with the infants left behind. I started an "expressed breast milk" clinic for these infants until I began wondering out loud how the hospital had cared for these infants prior to my arrival in Zorzor. That's when I discovered that the hospital community was simply humoring me, yet honoring my labor. They already were taking advantage of a well-known phenomenon. These infants, when put to the breast of the maternal grandmother, induced lactation and were successfully fed. I eventually found other projects that kept me at the hospital late most nights.

Zorzor was an isolated town with no television, so staff members would do plenty of reading and find creative ways to entertain ourselves in our "downtime." For example we would go to each other's houses and read a play out of a book—each person becoming a particular character.

Every month or so I would find a way to get back to Monrovia, where the government was still in turmoil. One of the reasons was to collect my pay cheque. I was still bent on building a house for my mother, and I had to procure the funds to make it a reality. While there was mail service to Zorzor, it was very unreliable.

If I was lucky, I would catch a ride with a missionary pilot who might happen by in a small Cessna 172, but that was rare. Most of the time I would make the trek in what we referred to as a "Kill Me Quick" taxi van. Most of the journey was on dirt roads, and I can't begin to count the times we were stuck in mud up to the axles—with rain-soaked passengers pulling and pushing the vehicle out of the muck and mire. I often referred to these vehicles as "Noah's Ark on wheels." I always stayed with my friend Marlayne at the Lutheran guesthouse, where I also had my mail delivered. The government was still in turmoil, and often I would get my pay cheques two months late.

On one of the early trips to Monrovia, I bumped into Dr. Mac at the Ministry of Health, which was adjacent to the Lutheran guesthouse. Marlayne invited him over and we had a wonderful time reminiscing about how we had first met when I was in medical school and he was a professor. He especially liked the palm wine and bush meat I had brought down from Zorzor to share with Marlayne. She started inviting him over for dinner whenever I was in town.

After my fourth trip to Monrovia, he said, "Glena, I have this great big house that I rent from the Mobil Oil Company, and nobody lives in it. Why don't you plan to stay there instead of coming to the guesthouse?"

While the guesthouse was a thoroughfare to meet people from different countries, Dr. Mac's house could afford me privacy and save me guesthouse fees.

Dr. Mac was the person who befriended my husband and tried to help me. All I really knew of him was that he was married and teaching pharmacology at the medical college. I soon learned that his wife had left him. On my next trip to Monrovia, I stayed at his home, but he was working, and we were never in the residence at the same time. It really made no difference.

The following month, I was back again. As I was cooking a meal for myself, Dr. Mac walked in, smiled, and exclaimed, "Oh, I guess I get some palm wine today!"

During the conversation that followed, tears welled in his eyes when he confided, "I am missing my wife." He also told me, "She developed cancer and moved back to the States. We will never be able to have children."

It was sad to see him sad. I had only known a laughing Dr. Mac up to this point.

Someone Who Cared

From that point on, our relationship changed from one of hello and good-bye to something moe personal. I had been aware that he knew quite a lot about me from being on the faculty committee that had discussed my marriage and separation from Kylkon. No longer was our conversation focused on palm wine and bush meat. It now conveyed a tone of "I care about you."

To be honest, we really enjoyed each other's company and had fun together. As part of our humor, I would pretend to be English (since I came from a British protectorate) and he would impersonate an Irishman (since that was his heritage), and we would banter back and forth, laughing hysterically. We connected intellectually. Over the many meals we shared together, I relayed how the training at JFK Hospital had not prepared me for some of the things I was seeing in Zorzor.

When I couldn't get to Monrovia, we began sending letters to each other via Noah's Ark. The topics were innocent enough. He wrote how he had purchased a used car. I answered, "When your contract is over and you return to the States, I'll buy it from you."

He had access to news of big city Monrovia and Sierra Leone and kept me up to date with the economy, the coup, and JFK Hospital. I would answer with paragraphs about how genuine and family-oriented the people of Zorzor were compared with those in the capital city. "You need to come up sometime and see for yourself," I wrote.

There was one period when Dr. Hove was on leave and I needed to cover for him at the hospital. That's when Dr. Mac suggested that he visit Zorzor.

While he was there, I asked him about our friendship.

"Why me?" I wanted to know.

"Well," he responded, "I love being in your company."

Oddly, I felt the same way.

It reached the point that whenever I saw Dr. Mac, my day just got better. He, however, suddenly started addressing me formally as "Dr. Davies."

When I asked him about it, he complained, "You always call me Dr. Mac. My name is John."

"Very well then, John," I replied.

If anyone had implied I was romantically involved with him, I would have called them a liar. To me, he was a dear friend—like a big brother. Tears about my past with Kylkon were beginning to dry up.

John shared with me more details of his wife's health and their separation.

Things began to take on a different tone when I found myself looking forward to letters from him.

Love Letters?

When I stayed at John's house in Monrovia, we would always sleep in separate bedrooms. But one time it had been raining, and there was a leak in the room where I slept. So he left a note saying, "In case you arrive, feel free to sleep in my bedroom," which I did.

About three o'clock in the morning I heard a car pull in the carport. When John opened the door of the bedroom, I pulled the covers tightly up to my neck.

"You must be wearing something fancy," he commented as he stood in the doorway. I usually slept in my scrubs, but that weekend I had brought something different. "Oh yeah," I answered, uncomfortably.

John walked over and, sitting on the edge of the bed, said, "You know, we've been writing to each other for quite a long time."

"That's true," I answered.

He continued, "Well, I think those are love letters."

This literally took my breath away. I could feel the air leave my body—and there was an uncomfortable silence.

John added, "You can pull the blanket up over you, or you can put it down. It makes no difference to me."

I wasn't shivering because I was cold; it actually was hot. I was trembling because I was scared at what was unfolding right before my eyes. I thought, *Oh, dear God. I hope I haven't misled him.*

He pulled the blanket away from my chin and tenderly whispered, "You don't have to worry."

My mind was spinning. *What in the world is going on? He is touching my clothing—something he has never done before.*

Then John said, "Glena, I love you."

I quietly responded, "Thank you." I honestly didn't know what else to say.

We talked and talked until we both fell asleep.

The next day we had lunch at a nearby restaurant run by a woman who knew how to cook Bitter Leaf really well. We began to discuss what had taken place the previous night, and John made the point,

"We can't deny that we slept in the same bed last night, even though nothing happened."

A Piece of the Puzzle

I was beset with gynecological issues from the onset of menarche. My mom said my paternal aunt had the same problems. I felt like the woman with the issue of blood mentioned in Luke 8:43—ten long days of menstrual flow coupled with short twenty-one-day cycles. The cramping pain made me sweat and feel faint. The resulting chronic anemia made my heart beat fast, but I wasn't a stranger to blood or pain.

In secondary school I consulted my classmates; their menstrual cycles were three to five days.

In college I had been diagnosed with possible endometriosis or fibroids. I declined any interventions because after ten days I was pain free and as good as could be. Fixing my bleeding issue was not a priority, but by the end of my intern year at JFK Hospital, nature forced me to pay attention. I had been bleeding continuously for about forty-five days, and I had become very anemic. Running up and down the hospital stairs became more difficult, and finally one day I collapsed.

During surgery the doctors found an enlarged, lobulated uterus about the size of a grapefruit and full of fibroids. They performed a myomectomy (removal of the fibroids), and ultimately the bleeding was contained. I had lost a lot of blood loss during the surgery, so a blood transfusion was required.

O-negative blood is rare—and rarer still on the West African coast. I had no family in Liberia, and the missionary community and medical school staff were urged to help find me a donor. Despite the low odds, a premed student and Karen, a Lutheran missionary nurse, were a perfect match.

Dr. Mac, on hearing the need for blood donations, promptly donated his B+ blood. He was, of course, not a match, but he stood outside the supermarket doors urging shoppers to donate blood. Of all the people who donated, only four O-negative persons were identified—and so began the registry of those with O-negative blood in Monrovia. We kept track of each other's whereabouts, because while we were universal donors, we could only receive blood from each other.

Just as I was about to be dismissed from the hospital, the doctor said, "The bleeding has stopped and your blood count is good. How do you feel?"

"Great," I replied, ready to jump out of bed.

Then the doctor continued, "Oh, by the way, we considered doing a hysterectomy, but we didn't."

"Why?" I wanted to know.

He answered, "Because you had fibroids everywhere, inside and on the outside of your uterus—what you have left now is flabby. Every site we removed a fibroid from will form a scar." He added, "With progressive healing your uterus will shrink, and it will be almost impossible for implantation of any future fetus to occur."

I heard and understood what he was telling me, but I had to ask him what that meant.

"Well," he continued, "It will be a miracle for you to ever get pregnant."

I sat there, motionless.

Then he added, "Even if you tried to conceive within the next three months, your chances are almost zero."

"Zero?" I questioned.

"No, not zero, but nearly zero," he said.

I needed sleep, and I tried to rest, but it didn't last long. I could hear the voice of my mother in my head, "But you have medicine."

They were the same words she spoke when I finally mustered the courage to tell her that my marriage had failed. It had angered me then. Since when did I agree to swap love, marriage, and children for *medicine*? I had agreed to medicine first—and then the other two.

"He Gets It"

I remember sitting across from John at the restaurant, staring blankly at him when he mentioned, "We slept in the same bed last night and nothing happened."

I replied, "You're right, nothing *will* happen." And I thought to myself, *But I have medicine, which is about all I will ever have.*

Those were the thoughts that had preoccupied my mind as we drove silently to his home.

"Listen," he said, "I will sleep in the other room tonight. I don't want you to be uncomfortable. That way nothing will happen."

I smiled and said, "You don't understand."

"What don't I understand?" he countered, as he led me to the couch and we sat down.

"Do you remember when you had that blood drive for me?" I asked him.

"Yes," he answered. "I've been wondering what was happening with that, but the last time I saw you, you were so excited about going to Zorzor, I didn't want to pry. So I didn't ask you about it." He paused, waiting for me to continue.

"The surgery I had . . ."

"Yes, go on."

"Well, they told me that my chances of ever becoming a mother was nearly zero."

"Zero?" he asked.

"No, not zero—*nearly* zero," I said.

We tossed around the word, and then I said, "If it's zero, at least I have medicine."

He questioned, "Why does it have to be a choice of exclusives? You love medicine and, yes, you will always have it, but you can and should be a mother—in fact, you'll make a wonderful mom."

I thought, *He gets it. At last somebody gets it.*

I gazed upward, as if God was hovering over us. *He gets it . . .*

My moment of silent joy was interrupted by his next statement. "But I pity the poor kid," he said, smiling.

"Why?" I asked.

"He will have to learn how to spell *discombobulated* by first grade, make rounds by the fifth grade, and carry his soccer ball and hockey stick in his lunch bag!"

We spent the rest of the evening laughing as we added things to the list that this imaginary child would have to accomplish, and by what age. Just before I got up to go to bed, he gave me a piece of paper. "Here," he said, "it's a blueprint for his lunch box." He had drawn one with compartments—a banana for potassium, a hat with a visor, and a small tube of sunscreen.

"What's this small compartment for?" I asked.

"For Tylenol," he smiled. "He will need it. His lunch box will weigh a ton with all the things his mother will make him carry." I laughed and went up to bed.

"John," I called down to him. "You don't have to sleep in the other bedroom."

I must have fallen asleep before my head hit the pillow. I woke up the next morning, and John was next to me.

"You were out like a light," he whispered.

"I'm sorry," I muttered.

Then he said, "I meant to tell you that I saw your old Histology teacher, Joe K, with his little boy on the Bushrod Island Bridge. They were fishing."

"Oh, yeah?" I responded.

Suddenly there was quiet, and I realized he was crying. "What's wrong?"

Through his tears, he said, "You should have seen them. Father and child. Now that's something I may never experience."

I started to cry too. When I started to speak, I couldn't. I knew exactly what I wanted to say, but the words stuck in my throat. The tears brought great relief. I lay there thinking, *What is happening to me? Why is John here?*

I silently prayed. *Too many puzzle pieces. God, how are all these pieces going to fit?*

In the quiet of the moment I heard myself say, "If we carry on like this, one of us might get pregnant."

"What are the chances of that happening?" he asked.

"Zero to nearly zero," I replied—and we both burst out laughing.

"So if it does happen, can I keep the baby?" I asked.

"Of course," he replied. "But it will be a miracle."

Worried About Tomorrow

I left for Zorzor that morning, full of emotion and questions. I felt comforted, but afraid. Had I just stepped off my "bus" and was now wandering off in uncharted territory? I comforted myself with a prayer as I rested in one of the seats of the "Kill Me Quick" vans. Thoughts danced in my head. *Is this the right thing to do? Why is John in my life? What will I say to my mother if... How will I tell Ken and Doris? What will my missionary friends think?*

Finally, weary of the recurring questions, a new thought came to my mind. It was from Matthew 6:34: *"Do not worry about tomorrow, for tomorrow will worry about its own things. Sufficient for the day is its own trouble."*

Normally when I made one of these "Noah's Ark, Kill Me Quick" trips, I would worry about the vehicle tipping over. This time I slept peacefully.

It was now semester break at the Medical College, and John visited Zorzor frequently. He toured the village, drank fresh palm wine, and when I finished working at the hospital, we took turns reading *The Thorn Birds* by Colleen McCullough out loud to each other.

One early morning we were rudely awakened by what sounded like a child in distress. It was the bleating of a goat in the backyard.

I tried unsuccessfully to open the back door, so I tried to go through the front door, but I walked directly into a huge basket of freshly harvested peanuts on the front porch. Then, as I walked around to the back door, I noticed another small basket full of eggs. And I found a very fat goat securely tied to the back door.

At the hospital I asked the staff about the baskets and the goat. They explained that several villagers who I had recently discharged had come back with the gifts.

I was dismayed to hear this. "So after all the time I spend in the clinic, teaching them about proper nutrition and telling them they should increase the protein in their children's diets, they turn around and give it to me?" I said.

One of the nurses replied, "Sister, they heard you, but they say they don't want to lose you."

"Why would they lose me?" I asked.

I didn't realize that I was much thinner than when I first arrived at Zorzor. I worked long hours, and I spent time walking to and from villagers homes making house calls when I could.

"If you don't want the gifts, we will help you eat them," one of the staff members replied—"especially that fat goat. But you will hurt their feelings."

"Okay then," I said.

My uterus was acting up again. I was in pain and didn't feel like trudging home for lunch. It was "Big Clinic Day," when villagers walk for miles from all over the Zorzor area to come for treatment. Women and children waited in one group in the shade while the men jostled each other for their position in line. They took turns standing on the scale and watching the needle's deflection. The further the needle swung, the older the man was presumed to be— and he got to stand at the head of the line.

I lay sprawled on one of the benches nearby, smiling to myself about their antics and not interfering.

One of the local aides startled me by interrupting my reverie. "Sister," she asked, "Are you circumcised?"

"No," I exclaimed. "Why?"

She continued, "My grandma would like to circumcise you."

"No. No thanks," I emphatically replied. There are some discussions, practices, or behaviors one does not engage in or encourage—and this was one of them.

Big Clinic Day was long and fatiguing that day, and my cramps didn't let up. My last patient was a very young woman in her third trimester, but her legs were swollen up to her knees. Her abdomen was very large, and I diagnosed her with polyhydramnios (excessive amniotic fluid). Now to find the cause of her excessive fluid; this was my favorite part of medicine. Perhaps the fetus had an anomaly, or the mother had diabetes, heart disease, or kidney disease. Maybe she would be having twins.

The woman noticed that I spent a long time examining her. "Sister, what's wrong?" she asked as I listened some more for the baby's heartbeat. Finally I looked up at her and said, "I think you are having twins!"

She sat up abruptly. "Twins?" She was so disappointed. "I am not a goat—goats have twins!"

I trudged home slowly, chastising God all the way. "This makes no sense. She is going to have twins and doesn't want them. I want children, and I get cramps."

Back and forth I made my case before God. "I haven't done anything to deserve this," I pleaded in that infantile way people do who have no understanding of God. "I go to church. I help other people . . ." On and on I went until the tears were streaming down my face. In a last act of defiance, I exclaimed, "Damn it. What do I have to do to please you, God, and the world?"

I can't explain what happened next, but I clearly heard the words, "Sing a new song."

Had I really heard a voice, or was I just scared that I said "damn it" to the Lord? In any case, I promised God how well I would take care of any child He gave me. Yes, I would teach him big words, and more. Then, with a big flourish, I said, "Here's the sign I will look for that will let me know You have heard me and agreed with me. If You let me have a child with John, and then if no one gives me flack about it, I will know You approve."

To this day it seems uncanny to me the latitude the mind will allow the body just so it gets what it wants.

The Jug with a Broken Lip

As I walked up to the house, I saw John on the porch feeding the goat some bread. "Where did this puddle come from?" I asked him.

"Oh, I washed the goat," he said. "She's a girl."

"Then I'll name her Frieda," I suggested.

"Looks like you had a hard day," John said.

"No harder than any other," I responded.

"You can't fool me. You've been crying."

Other than Grandmother Constance, who at a glance could see my joy, anxiety, or worry, John was the only other person who could "read" me like that. I told him about the mom-to-be and her reaction to the news she was carrying twins.

"Is that why you were crying?"

"Duh!" I replied. "It's not fair, is it?" I burst into another tirade of how "unfair" all this was.

John was quiet. "You look tired," he said.

"I've got cramps," I answered.

"That again?" he asked.

"Yes."

"Let me see, it's been about a year or so since your surgery," he commented.

"Yep."

"So you're well past the three-month window of 'nearly zero.'"

A PLACE CALLED ZORZOR

I responded, "I'm in the zero zone now, I think."
"You should go down to JFK hospital and check things out."

The next morning as I stepped out to leave for the clinic in Zorzor, there was a woman sitting on the porch. When she saw me, she smiled and offered me a clay jug. She didn't speak English, but she clearly had something to tell me.

I flagged down one of the nursing students who was passing by. "What is she saying?" I asked, hoping she could translate.

"She wants to thank you for saving her life."

"I've never seen this woman before," I said.

"Yes, you have. She says she was so sick with a high fever after her baby was born about a month ago that she couldn't walk to the clinic, but she sent word and you came. She explained further that you found that she had a huge breast abscess which you drained, and then you gave her a shot and some pills. She wants to show you her breast and explain something about the jug she made for you."

With that, the woman lifted her blouse. Her breast had healed completely, but there was a scar on one side of the nipple that distorted it. She then explained that she was very good at making pottery, but she made this jug with a crooked lip to deliberately remind me of her.

I had fixed her breast, which now had a crooked nipple, so she made me a jug with a crooked lip. Not all comedians are in Hollywood!

When I hugged and thanked her, she burst out crying. "They were going to let me lay on a mat and die. But you came."

I assured her that I was just doing my job.

Until I left Zorzor, the porch was the place where patients left hammocks, country cloths, and food to show their appreciation. These people were not rich in material things, but they were rich in spirit because they showed gratitude—even for small things.

Waiting for the Results

The days in Zorzor were long and slow. Medical exchange students from Ireland, Germany, the United States, and Peace Corps workers came and went. Many taught at the nursing school. Dr. Hove and I were invited to give guest lectures at the nursing school in Zorzor, so my trips to Monrovia became less frequent.

I had reached the halfway point in my rural service obligation and was getting excited about finally going to Sierra Leone to practice medicine.

John and I wrote to each other daily. He had exam papers to grade, I was getting busier by the day, and the road between Zorzor and Monrovia often was so washed out that travel was impossible. We relied on "Noah's Ark" for mail delivery.

In one letter I told John, "I have just become a grandmother!" Frieda wasn't a fat goat after all. She was pregnant and delivered a baby goat—which entitled me to that name!

John's letters were hysterically funny, but they almost always ended with something such as, "It seems like a morgue around here without you."

One day, there he was, standing in my doorway in Zorzor. I had come home early from my rounds due to severe pelvic cramps.

"You can't live like this," he complained.

I agreed and went to JFK Hospital in Monrovia for a laparoscopy. Nothing spectacular was found, although there were new fibroids. My odds had not changed.

As the rains diminished, the roads became more pliable, and a few times I showed up at his door without forewarning. I felt respected, loved, and very comfortable. The humiliation and pain Kylkon had caused me was receding.

When John spoke of his wife, he cried, and I gave him room to grieve. I have yet to meet another person whose sensibilities matched mine as his did.

The weeks rolled by, and the routine at Zorzor became easier. By late October, although the workload lessened, I was much more fatigued. Then I fainted in the operating room—and I fainted again two days later during rounds. I was given a few days off to rest, but I hitched a ride to Monrovia to visit John. As I left to return back to Zorzor, I told him I would get a pregnancy test.

To protect my confidentiality, I put a Jane Doe-like Liberian name on the sample I submitted. When the results came back, I walked around for two days in disbelief.

Then I sent John a letter. In the middle of the second page I embedded the words, "HCG positive," and ended by saying, "See you next week."

CHAPTER FOURTEEN

SHIFTING SANDS

The year 1984 was drawing to a close.

My marriage had ended (I was just waiting for official paperwork), and my seven years in Liberia were just about over. I left Zorzor tearfully, but grateful for the experience. Before leaving, I auctioned Frieda off in a raffle to raise funds for the hospital.

My fear of being childless had ended with my pregnancy. I summoned the courage to inform my mother, Ken and Doris, and by extension, the First Baptist family, and a handful of my Lutheran missionary friends who I swore to secrecy. No one asked any questions or judged me. Everyone seemed to be genuinely happy with the news.

I was approaching my thirty-fifth birthday. *Better late than never,* I joked to myself.

New beginnings beckoned. I was singing a new song, anxious to get to Freetown to start practicing—and looking forward to see the land I bought to get my mother out of the roach- and rat-infested house we had all known as home. And, of course, I was eager for motherhood. I couldn't ask the universe for more.

It was all so perfect, especially since I believed God was the architect of this plan.

John and I were inseparable. We talked about life's joys and heartaches. He knew I was still raw just beneath the surface, and I knew he was in turmoil about his marriage, so we skirted any talk of marriage with each other.

I don't remember exactly when we started calling each other "blood brothers." It was likely after the blood drive. Just about everything John did seemed to be for my benefit. We had enough separate interests that we were just as happy together or apart, enjoying other activities. He was an avid golfer, I read and walked on the beach, and we took short day trips. We also had things to sort out regarding our immediate future.

I thought, *Our deep affection for one other will be the glue that keeps us together. Furthermore, our genes, through this child, will be entwined through time . . . so what's the rush? What is there to worry about?* I was secure in the simplistic "belief system" I had created for myself.

I reasoned that individuals self-select who they associate with or even become. You even see it as early as in high school. The jocks cluster together, the bookworms knuckle down and study together, the clowns and cutups end up in detention together, and the dishonest ones continue in the behaviors that ultimately land them in jail—and they become jailbirds together.

By the same token, people who want a better world create such things as medicine to help themselves and others. They become teachers and write books so we can learn and discover. They become farmers and gardeners to grow crops to feed mankind and all of God's creatures. They become lawyers, justices, and legislators who make and enforce laws to protect the rights and dignity of humanity and the world. This is the order that God intended. *Good things happened to good people*, so said my not-so-well-developed brain as it continued to drive and direct my beliefs.

As with most earthquakes, first comes the rumbling, followed by the crack, and finally the crash.

Years earlier, Jim Dick, pastor at First Baptist in Waukesha, and I had had healthy debates while I was waiting to go to Michigan State University. I had insisted that there had to be a reason why bad things happened to good people, implying some measure of culpability. I told him, "If you just stay on the bus as a passenger and let God drive, you'll be safe. He loves us and takes care of us." Then I quoted Luke 12:27: "Consider the lilies, how they grow: they neither toil or spin" and how our heavenly Father cares for them.

Pastor Dick shot back, "So a good man's wife dies of breast cancer. Is it His fault? A child dies; is it the parents' fault?"

The rumblings of my world had begun, but there were no cracks. I didn't have an explanation, but I was willing to search.

Then 1985 happened.

Choices and Risks

We had survived the coup d'ètat of Liberia in 1980, yet the underpinnings for further unrest had been firmly established. The infrastructure was beginning to crumble, but everyone went about putting their lives back together as best as they could.

I was now packing up my prized possessions and sending them to Freetown, especially the gifts that had been handmade for me in Zorzor. The evenings were cool, so John and I sat outside and enjoyed each other's company, trying not to worry. I was also waiting for my clearance papers from the Ministry of Health and my exit visa which would enable me to leave Liberia permanently.

John was the first to get a fever—so high that he was delirious.

Three days later I started to shiver. We both had malaria. Since there was suspicion that chloroquine-resistant malaria was now in Liberia, a doctor at JFK gave me a choice between two antimalarial medicines. I was told, "You can either take chloroquine, with the risk that it may not work and you and your baby might get very sick, or you can take Fansidar and you will certainly get better, but it can cause possible birth defects."

I knew I wasn't about to take a medication that would cause any harm to my child, so I told John, "You take the Fansidar, I'll take the chloroquine." He agreed.

Two days later I was admitted to JFK with what they presumed was Stevens-Johnson Syndrome and premature rupture of membranes. I remained bedridden for the next five months until our baby was born on May 7. I named him Sean for his father John and my brother Ian.

The chloroquine worked, but I had a severe reaction to the drug. My missionary friends rallied and cared for Sean, even breastfeeding him.

The Unexpected Stopover

As the infrastructure of Liberia began to crack and crumble, so did my well-laid plans. When I was finally discharged from the hospital, Sean and I could not return to John's house because electricity and water were being rationed city-wide. The Lutherans had their own generators and water supply, so Jeannette, a Lutheran missionary nurse and midwife, invited Sean and I to stay in her home. She breastfed Sean when I was still too weak. But I was glad that my hair was growing back and my skin, which would peel at the slightest touch, was beginning to stop shedding. Sean didn't fare too well, and I cried uncontrollably.

There were no pediatricians in town, so John purchased a plane ticket for me to take Sean to the United States for medical treatment. It seemed everyone we knew was committed to caring for us. Margo Schleman, an American pediatric cardiologiost who had been one of my teachers at the Medical School, returned home sometime after the coup d'ètat. She picked us up a the airport in New York and took us to Temple University Hospital in Philadelphia, where Sean was treated. Within two weeks he was much improved, so I took the opportunity to see my sister, Olive, in Virginia, Marlayne in New Jersey, and all our friends in Wisconsin. Everyone thought he was *so* cute. I was relieved and grateful that Sean was healthy and thriving.

On our return to Liberia, I decided to stop in Freetown to see my mom, finalize all matters with the purchased land, and start preparations for building something on the property for me, Sean, and my mom, with plans to later expand it into a clinic.

The stopover was fortuitous. All hell broke out in Liberia. Little did we know then that the crack would spread into Sierra Leone, decimating more than a quarter million lives and displacing 2.5 million people. The resentment that had formented in the Liberian coup was now stirring in my home country. Was it really providential, or was I still on the bus?

Sisi's house in Freetown had deteriorated further. The seasonal rains caused the wood to swell and rot, and the back door had eventually fallen off. No safety was guaranteed. The cockroaches in the latrine had joined forces with the mice and rats, and when the mosquitos joined in, it was a perfect setup for misery.

Dissent in Sierra Leone was spreading just as quickly as the infrastructure was crumbling. At first I could get around by taxi, trying to find Dr. Cole regarding the land. I took Sean with me wherever I went—he was noticed and known as the cute baby with red hair.

Next, I took to casing out Dr. Cole's clinic, and then his home—all to no avail. When the country ran out of petrol, it became increasingly difficult for me to hunt down Dr. Cole, but I continued to try.

I walked to wherever I thought I could find him. Finally one day I decided to camp out at his house. Many hours later he appeared in the living room, grinning: "Glena, it's so good to see you!"

I could barely contain my disdain. I busied myself with breastfeeding Sean, deliberately creating an awkward silence. Finally I told him that I had spent several weeks trying to find him. Then I said, "I would like the deed to my property today . . . so I can start building."

"The papers are not yet in order," he answered, "but if you are looking for a place to stay, I own an apartment building downtown. Let me show it to you."

He drove me to the place, which was really dilapidated. "No, this won't work. I want what I paid for."

The next day I returned to his house and told Mrs. Cole, "I am waiting to take my mother to the land I bought. I need to show her where I plan to build a clinic and a home for us." She was friendly, but evasive. "Well, we are fixing up a place where our two daughters will live when they come back from England. One side needs a little quick work. Maybe my husband will let you stay there until the paperwork is finished on your property."

When I went to see what they were offering, it was a mess, needing much more than a little "quick work." A watchman was stationed outside to make sure nobody stole the construction materials. It also needed screens on the windows and locks on the doors, but at least it had running water. So I decided to move in with my baby.

I brought my mother over and, with a furrowed brow, she exclaimed, "Is this what you were going to surprise me with?"

I assured her the dwelling was only temporary.

A Change of Plans

Something wasn't right. I was between despair and distraught. I kept my ear glued to the transistor radio that was always on. Sometimes there would be a blurb from the BBC (British Broadcasting Corporation) or VOA (Voice of America) with coverage of a second coup underway in Liberia.

Five years earlier President Tolbert had been overthrown and executed by the rebel forces of Samuel K. Doe, who was now in charge. The country was being run by his People's Redemption Council, and the country was badly divided. Doe came from the minority Krahn tribe and placed all of his friends in power. Other tribes, particularly the Mano and Gio, charged him with corruption, which led to one of the bloodiest wars on the African continent.

The wheels were slowly coming off my bus. The sentiment on the streets was that Sierra Leone was rife for its own meltdown. I was now spending all my time and the money I had saved to build the house on food, transportation, and, when available, communications. I frequented both the Liberian and American embassies. I sent telegrams and waited in long lines to access the international phone system, which was now only available at the Sierra Leone Telecommunications building in downtown Freetown.

Then one day I heard on the radio that President Doe had issued an order for all essential personnel to return to Liberia. The plans I had been working on for my transition to Freetown were foiled by my five-month hospitalization and subsequent travel to the USA.

When it was time to return, I arranged my return ticket first to go to Monrovia to take care of all the loose ends and find out what was happening to John. Technically I considered myself still an employee of the Ministry of Health—therefore a member of the "essential personnel."

Fearing that by now most governments either would have ordered their citizens (expatriates) to return home or moved them to safety in this quickly deteriorating situation, I hoped to collect my clearance papers from the Ministry of Health and find some letter or instruction from John. With this in mind, I went to the border to report as "essential personnel."

"Give me your passport," the customs official demanded. I handed him my Booklet of Permanent Residency to Liberia.

"Passport!" he barked again.

I don't know what came over me, but instinctively I sensed that parting with my passport would be life-altering. I decided that this guy could not be trusted; perhaps it was the way he peppered me with questions. There was no mistaking the feeling of foreboding in the pit of my stomach. So when he said, "You can't come in," I simply turned away with my passport tucked in my bra.

In just a few short days the Liberian-Sierra Leone border was sealed. Many of the Sierra Leoneans who had crossed days or weeks before my attempt were never seen or heard from again. Most were accused of harboring or helping the coup plotters. Americans and Sierra Leonians were suspect.

I sometimes wonder about my fate had I crossed the border that day. I surely had fraternized with my fair share of Americans and Liberians, including the Minister of Finance, Ellen Johnson Sirleaf, who was now under arrest.

By now, I convinced myself that John would not have remained in Liberia. He probably would be in the United States—but where?

Checking in with God

The situation in Sierra Leone was becoming similar to holding a piece of chocolate in your sweaty palm on a hot day. You still have it, but it's messy. The rule of law in Freetown was now a distant memory.

Dr. Cole never produced the deed or ever showed me the land. My mother, sensing chicanery, resigned herself to living out her days at our home on Waterloo Street.

Water, electricity, petrol, and mail delivery became more and more sporadic. Alone and afraid, I tried to check in with God. This time it seemed that all the wheels had fallen off the bus. Where could I turn? I told myself, *If you let God do the driving, you won't get lost—just stalled like one of those "Kill Me Quick" vans.* I still could laugh at anything.

Early the next morning I was awakened by my mother, who had walked the nearly five miles to the house I was temporarily staying in.

Oh, God, I thought. *This has to be bad.*

It was just after 7:00 a.m. My heart was pounding.

"You received a telegram," she said.

"Is it from Olive? The Steeles? John?" I asked.

"Open it," she shrieked. There was no way to tell where the telegram originated from, or when it had been sent. All it contained were the words, "Do not travel to Liberia. U.S.? JJ."

It was from John.

I grabbed Sean and rushed to the American embassy. I took every document I had, including my passport, which showed my recent visa stamp to the U.S., a passport-size picture of John, and a few of his letters that I always carried with me. The letters were my instant replay—just like reruns of old American television sitcoms.

I decided to await my turn in the slowly moving line outside the embassy doors. Once I got past the entrance and the embassy staff discovered I was a physician, I would never have to stand in line again. By now, Sean was even cuter, and he smiled and charmed everyone.

Finally it was my turn. The interview was very long, very personal, and very detailed. "So where is John?" the interviewer, a woman, asked me.

"That is exactly what I am trying to find out," I replied. "His son, Sean, and I are anxious to see him. We have just returned from the States, and we were planning to go to Monrovia." I produced the unused portion of the plane ticket I still had.

More and more questions. "So where is the ticket to get you and your son to the USA?"

"I don't have one yet. I am trying to reconnect with John. He works for the WHO (World Health Organization). I am sure he knows I am trying to reach him."

The embassy staff was very helpful. "You're not alone in this situation," they assured me. "Several people are having tickets sent to this embassy from their relatives in the U.S. Perhaps he could send it here."

"But I don't know where he is," I answered.

"You're married to him, and you don't know his U.S. address?"

This triggered another barrage of questions that were even more personal. "No, I never said we were married. I met him in Liberia, and, yes, he and I have this little guy."

"So your son is illegitimate?"

"Yes," I said, wincing.

"So what will you do once you get to the U.S.?"

Before I could answer, she said, "You could take the ECFMG (Educational Commission for Foreign Medical Graduates) exam, the visa qualifying exam, and continue to study in the U.S. until things settle down in Liberia and Sierra Leone."

My mother was right. I always have medicine.

Facing an Uncertain Ocean

When I was able, I sent telegrams to everyone I knew in America. Finally one day there were two tickets waiting for me at the U.S. embassy. One from Marlayne with a short note: "Pay me back when you can." The other was from the First Baptist Church in Waukesha. It read, "See you soon."

I exhaled, long and hard. I didn't cry—I was too relieved for tears. But as I walked down Trelawney Street and faced the Atlantic Ocean, in my mind's eye, I was seeing my ancestors on the beach, looking west . . . facing the same ocean shackled in chains, bound for America, in despair, not knowing what awaited them.

In a split frame, here they were again. Now facing east on the Nova Scotia shores, unchained physically, but bound by poverty and degradation, eager to arrive on Africa's shores, hopeful!

It was as if I were at Freetown's Lungi airport again, back in September 1971. The Harmattan—a dry, dusty eastern wind on the West African coast—had not officially started yet, but the wind was sharp across my face. I was eager to shed the indignity and shame my father had heaped on my mother. I wanted to escape the constant foraging my mother had to endure to provide for her children. My life had to be different. I had to help myself, and others. I had hope. I would cross those waters without chains.

Sean started to cry. I had to find somewhere to sit and breastfeed him, so I walked a few steps toward the Cotton Tree. The embassy wasn't very far away. I found a shady spot and kept my face westward, toward the Atlantic.

I am going back to America, I kept telling myself. I was hopeful but fearful. *But you don't know what you are going to do,* my mind kept repeating. *I know,* I answered myself. *They went not knowing where they were going—and in chains! They had no choice. They didn't know what to expect either.*

By the time I reached home that day, I was very apprehensive, with just enough anxiety to keep me staring at the ceiling. Eventually exhaustion carried me to sleep— the only place I could go without worry.

In less than a month I had my passport stamped with a six-month tourist visa. I was bound for America. I was going west, crossing the Atlantic Ocean.

An Uncomfortable Position

It was December 1985, a few days before my thirty-fifth birthday. Sean was now seven months old.

We had arrived in the U.S. safely, although I had been detained at the Lungi airport and separated from Sean. He had been cleared to board, and a stewardess had taken him. I was still being questioned, this time by Sierra Leone officials. The rule of law was nowhere to be found.

"Do you have diamonds?" they pressed. "Where are you hiding the diamonds? We have to search you." This went on for an hour, then another. "We have to take you back to Freetown."

Then I heard the plane's engines roaring, readying for takeoff.

"My baby is on that plane," I screamed.

The ferry from Lungi airport to Freetown had already left, carrying my mother and brother who had accompanied me to say good-bye.

"Oh, look, dollar bills," said one of the female officers as she searched my blue jean pockets. It was the same hundred dollar bill that Doris had pressed into my hands. "From the church," she said as I left Wisconsin with Sean just a few months earlier. "Just in case," she commented. "Traveling with a young child, you never know."

I stared at the officer without seeing her. I wasn't sure what would happen next. As calmly as I could, I told her how the money ended up in my back pocket. "I wasn't trying to hide it," I assured her.

"But you didn't declare it," she fired back.

"I never got through customs. You came and pulled me out of line before I could declare it," I told her.

The customs officials conferred for what seemed to be an eternity. Then one of them gruffly told me, "Get your creole ass out of here." He handed me the hundred dollar bill. I was escorted to the plane, which was still on the tarmac.

I hugged Sean and took my seat. Finally we were going to America. I had no idea what awaited me, but that day I was happy to leave the land of my birth—the land of diamonds—the land I loved.

We were supposed to fly to New York but ended up in Amsterdam, where we were met by officials and questioned about the interrogation at the Lungi airport—however, this team was very courteous and helpful. From there it was an uneventful nonstop flight to New York.

Kaplan Days

At the Steele's, the arrangement was the same as it had been years before. I pulled my weight by cleaning, cooking, and doing household chores, and they provided a roof over my head. The members at the Baptist church welcomed Sean and me with open arms.

The people in Wisconsin had been generous to me through the years, even though I had never, ever asked them for one penny. And this was not about to change.

I continued to send letters to John, but I never heard a word in return. I thought about him morning, noon, and night.

Sean was seven months old when we arrived. Now, at nine months, he was crawling on the floor, then sitting, standing, and grabbing everything in sight at the Steele's house. They didn't complain, but I could tell that having an active baby around was more than they had bargained for.

I had to find a way to extend my six-month visa.

Enrolling in the Kaplan University preparatory study course offered me that opportunity. It helped me prepare for the ECFMG exam.

Thankfully the church remained supportive of me and Sean. The Kaplan course fees were paid, Doris babysat Sean, and eventually Joanne and Glenice alternated days with Doris to give her a much-needed break. Frank and Marylou taught me how to drive, and on most weekends they invited us to their home to give Ken and Doris some space. All of these people were First Baptist church members, where "community" was not just a word, but a practice.

Frank taught shop and drivers ed at the local high school. "You need a car," he said. He was an expert with used vehicles. Soon I was the owner of a multicolored, mostly green "Chimera"—the only one in the world. It was part Chevy, part Oldsmobile, and part Ford. It worked very well most of the time, and when it needed repairs, Frank took it to the shop to teach his students.

In no time I was a licensed driver. Now I could stay later in the morning to take care of Sean instead of catching the bus from Pewaukee to Milwaukee, which meant that Ken had to drive me to the bus station and Doris would have to watch Sean. This liberated almost everyone involved in the Glena Project—no one needed to transport us, and I could now do odd jobs for some church members for meals or a little spending money. I could also use the resources at the local hospital library, which helped me cover more study course material.

When someone would ask about my ability to cope with Wisconsin's frigid weather, I would often think to myself, *The people here have embraced me so tightly with love that I am never cold!*

For me, however, there was an increasing despondency. My situation of almost complete dependency was eating away at every piece of dignity I had left. What happened to "most likely to succeed" Glena?

As the nights lengthened, so did the depths of my despair. The news reports of Liberia, and particularly Zorzor, that I gleaned from my missionary friends were dismal. It was nothing but stories of carnage. News of Sierra Leone was equally disturbing. Sometimes it was just easier not to know.

"What? Four Years?"

The course at Kaplan University was self-paced and self-tutored with practice test questions. I would try to get through as much material as possible, and then, once Sean was asleep, I could review the notes I made from the material that day.

At Kaplan, I hardly looked up or around me. When I did, I saw doctors from all over the globe—Greece, China, Cameroon, Philippines, India. It was a mini-United Nations, just has it had been in medical school.

Occasionally I would stand just outside the doors to stretch and take a break. Others did too. "You look new around here," one female student said. I learned she was a Filipino doctor.

"Yes," I replied. "I've been coming daily for two months now."

"This is my second year here," she commented. "Jerome over there has almost made it. Last year he got a 69. You know you have to get a 70 to pass. And Sonia has been coming for four years," she continued and burst out laughing.

"What? Four years?" I exclaimed. She beckoned Sonia to join us.

"So where are you from? Africa or something?" Sonia asked. She must have surmised that I had paddled straight from the jungles of Africa, and the only thing missing was a bone through my nose!

I didn't blame her; I looked the part. While I endeavored to keep my hygiene a priority, fashion and I had gone our separate ways.

She talked about how the exams seemed to get increasingly harder every year. I didn't need to hear more—I was anxious enough as it was.

The weeks went by quickly. After paying six hundred dollars for my car, I was determined to pay for the registration of the exam. I also decided to eat just one meal a day at Ken and Doris'. I knew it took a little pressure off them, and it kept me sharply focused on the one goal I had to achieve—passing the exam!

Sonia stopped me once to tell me that while I was outside stretching, she had looked at my notes. "Those are pretty good," she said. "If you let me xerox them I will give you twenty dollars."

This would mean more money for gas, diapers, toothpaste. I agreed. Ultimately word got around about my notes. The Filipino doctor suggested that we form a study group, but first she asked, "Does your husband have a job?"

"I'm not married," I replied.

When she talked about a study group, I told her I had to leave by 5:30 p.m. to pick up my son. She paused for a moment and then said, "I watch you, and you never eat anything from the time you get here until the time you leave."

She struck a nerve. I walked back to my booth, thinking, *If she spent more time studying, perhaps she wouldn't have to spend two years here.* I fought back the tears. She had broken my concentration; in fact, I was angry. As I packed up to leave for the day, she followed me. "I'm sorry," she said. "I used to be a social worker in my country before I became a doctor. I watch people; you look very sad. But I have seen your notes, and they are excellent. Even your 'Ingwish' is better than mine. What happened?"

I told her that I had studied in Liberia, but with the coup now turned in to war, I could not work there.

"Come with me to Fr. Gene, he can help you," she offered.

Reluctantly, I drove with her and met Fr. Gene, a Jesuit priest who didn't ask many questions. He just said, "Would twenty dollars a week help you?"

It was exactly what I needed. I cut out coupons for diapers from the Sunday paper, bought frozen turkey drumsticks when they went on sale, and continued to clean houses for church members.

One day I went to see Fr. Gene. He gave me the twenty dollars and then offered me some donated clothes.

"Thank you," I said. But I thought, *All I need is to pass this exam.*

He had more questions in his eyes than he asked, so I added, "Fr. Gene, I am having a difficult time right now, but it will soon be better."

He accepted that and said, "See you next week."

If I was tired enough, I could fall right to sleep, but I made myself review each day's lesson before slipping into bed.

I Can't Do This Anymore

As the exam date drew closer, I was overcome with anxiety. I felt worthless. Instead of counting my blessings, I entertained the "what ifs." *What if I failed the exam? What if Sean got sick? What if I got sick?* I would follow this by recounting my list of failures: *in my mid-thirties, failed marriage, unwed mother.*

I deliberately kept communication with my biological family to a minimum. Any news of my brother and mother in Freetown was unsettling. I had no money for long-distance calls to my sister Olive in Virginia, and writing to my sister Gloria in England was out of the question; I could not spare the money for stamps. What news would I share with them anyhow?

Before, I could pray and ask God to be the driver of my life and I would feel somewhat secure. But now I was increasingly doubtful of my ability to pass the exam. I withdrew from the study group, mostly because it became a socializing event, first at a Greek guy's penthouse, then at Sonia's place. Besides, I had nowhere to invite them to. Fewer and fewer contributed their summary notes, and I began splitting my days between the Kaplan site and the hospital library. I saw a lot of the Family Medicine residents dart about busily, and I would stare longingly at them and then chastize myself for thinking I could do this.

Even the words I thought were God's words of reassurance— "Glena, I am the driver, and you are the passenger. Just trust Me"— began to ring hollow.

"Trust Me"? That's all You've got? I don't have forever like You. My

time is limited. I can't take this exam more than once. I can't keep living like this.

The sleep that provided escape was now evasive. Sleepless, tired, and agitated, my thoughts became singular: *I have to get out of this. It's like kicking a stone wall. All I am going to get is broken toes. I want to quit—I will quit!*

Each passing day brought more despair.

I was beginning to be preoccupied with the thought of prolonged sleep. How can I sleep forever without going through the humiliation of failing this exam? Any thought of "but you have medicine" only enraged me. All I wanted now was to run away.

Once in a while I would go outside before anyone awakened to get the newspaper. It would be very quiet, except for a car going more than the posted 50 mph speed limit.

And then one morning, I thought, *That's it!* I'd hatched a plan.

The next morning, as I walked out to pick up the Steele's newspaper, I planned my last steps: *I will choose a car that is approaching at a very high speed. Then I will wait until it is close enough that the driver can't stop—and I will jump out in front of it!*

CHAPTER FIFTEEN

THE MATCH GAME

Standing at the edge of busy Highway SS in Pewaukee, I was about to do the unimaginable. Yet, caught in the throes of depression, I couldn't think of any other way out.

Cars were whizzing by. *If I dart in front of the next car, it will be over!* Then I heard a voice clearly say, "Why would you do that to Sean?" In my shaken state, I panicked and thought, *Oh my God. What is wrong with me?*

I ran back into the house, picked up my baby, clutched him tightly, and cried. My mind flashed back to the night my father totally humiliated my mother in front of our family. I was only thirteen years old at the time, but I remembered making the decision that no man would ever do such a thing to me.

So the first war I took on was my mother's fight. But now I was in my own battle. *Why would you leave your son a legacy of abandonment?* It was the cold water slap to the face I needed.

Something inside me began to ignite. It was almost as if the dying embers of my hopes and dreams were smoldering, and I needed to take bellows and pump air into them so the fire would flame up once more. I could feel the burning in the center of my being.

Every pore in my body was crying out, "Now go and get this exam over with—and make it into residency."

One of the women from the church who had been taking care of Sean on alternate days told me that she could no longer continue to babysit. With this pressing on my mind, as I was driving down the road, I saw a sign that read "Day Care." I drove in. With the well-worn clothes I was wearing, the woman behind the glass enclosure must have thought I was either homeless or destitute. After looking askance at me, she stepped out into the lobby and inquired, "How can I help you?"

"Can we talk privately?" I asked.

She led me into a small office and introduced herself as the owner. Her name was Elaine. My voice cracked as I told her, "I have a medical degree from overseas, but for me to practice in this country, I have to pass the American exam." Then I quickly added, "I have a young son, and I am looking for a place where I can trust that he will be safe two days a week while I study."

I continued, "I have absolutely no money, but I will sign a contract with you that when I pass my exam and am making a living, I will pay you for every day he is here."

Elaine paused for a moment, and then asked, "Where is he today?"

"One of our church members has him, but she can't keep him every day." I continued, "If you can find it in your heart to do this, you will find that he is a very good boy and won't be any trouble. I will drop him off and pick him up on time, bring the diapers, and a container of vegetables for him to eat."

At that point I couldn't hold back my tears. "I know this situation doesn't happen to everybody, but this is where I find myself."

"No one has ever asked me to do anything like this before," Elaine hesitatingly replied, "but, yes, I will help you."

The Moment I Had Been Waiting for

The day was finally here, and it was time to take the preclinical part of the ECFMG exam. Photo and fingerprint identification were required to enter the exam hall.

Having learned that the failing rate for international students was around 80 percent, I encouraged myself by thinking, *Well, 20 percent is better than zero.* I had dealt with odds before.

Someone suggested that our study group stay at one of the member's large apartment overnight so we could do some last minute cramming and travel to the exam location together so no one would be late.

I arranged for Sean to spend the night with a church member, and I joined the group. When we reached the test site, the registrar screened each of us very carefully. However, he waived Sonia right in. I learned later that she had failed the test so many times, they knew her by sight!

I took my place in the exam room and sat there in an almost trancelike state, thinking, *This is the moment I have been waiting for. This is it!* I closed my eyes and silently prayed, "Please, God, don't let me be like Sonia. Whatever I am doing today, may it be You who is writing the answers. Guide me. I just want to be the conduit."

During the test, I was sweating bullets!

After the exam, our study group met in the hallway, and a fellow named Angelo blurted out, "Only a genius can pass that test. With some of the questions, I honestly didn't know what the hell they were talking about!"

It would be weeks before the much-awaited results were announced. Of course, people at the church were pestering me with questions: "How do you feel about it? Do you think you passed?"

I laughed it off, saying, "Well, they say only a genius can pass that test, and I'm no genius. So we'll have to wait and see."

I knew the passing score was 70. *A 90 would be great,* I thought, *but I will easily settle for 80.* I daydreamed and prayed daily during the waiting time. I decided a score of 82 would be the sure sign that all would be well.

I could not register at Kaplan for the Clinical Modules without knowing my test results. Failing would require reregistering for the Preclinical Module I had just completed. I didn't have money for that, and I was determined not to ask anyone for the funds.

Kaplan was anxious for people to register early for the Clinical Modules, and they offered a 20 percent discount for payment in advance of the test result. However, there would be no refund if a person had failed and the advance payment for the Clinical Modules could not be applied to retake the Preclinical Modules.

On faith, I registered. If others believed in me, so would I.

Would She Call My Name?

On the day the results of the preclinical test were due to come in the mail, I was a nervous wreck. My aversion to opening mail of any kind surfaced.

I told Doris I would drive to Kaplan and wait for the results there. The mail in Pewaukee did not arrive until 4:00 p.m. I would rather go elsewhere to squirm.

"But your mail comes here," she said.

"I know," I replied. "*You* are going to have to open the envelope.

THE MATCH GAME

If I score 82 or better call Kathy, the lady at the Kaplan office. Here is her number. Ask for me, then ask her to just say my name out loud as though she was calling me to her office. That will be my cue that I passed, and I will hurry home."

She agreed. I drove to Kaplan, checked out a few Preclinical Modules, and sat near Kathy's window.

Angelo came in about 10:30. I couldn't read his expression. He went straight to Kathy's window. "I want to register for the Preclinical Module," he announced. He knew I overheard him. Then he added, "Sonia is on her way too."

He grinned—and we both burst out laughing.

"Did you register?" he asked me.

"Yes, last week—for the Clinical."

"So you lost your money then?" Angelo commented.

I replied, "I don't know yet. My mail doesn't come until four o'clock."

He looked down and saw the Preclinical Modules I had checked out. "What are you doing with those then?" he wanted to know.

Per the Kaplan contract, any number of modules could be checked out right up to the close of business on results day. If I failed the Preclinical Module, I wouldn't have access to them the next day without paying for them again, so I thought I would review as many of them as I could . . . just in case.

Angelo chuckled. "Don't check out so many. They'll all be here tomorrow. Pace yourself." As he walked past me to find a seat, Maria, the Filipino doctor, came in and registered. She spoke to no one and left. By mid-afternoon Jerome from Cameroon arrived. "I'm so close. I can't give up now," he announced.

"How close?" I asked.

"I got a 69 again," he answered.

My heart sank. Any hope I had until then was quickly fading, and my stomach was doing somersaults. I tried to stay busy by timing myself on a few practice tests.

Then it was four o'clock. I looked down at the practice test for what seemed like a long while. But when I glanced up at the clock again, it was only 4:01. I thought, *At this pace, this day will never end.*

I started another practice test but could not concentrate. So I stepped out to talk to Jerome, who was standing by the doorway. "Glena, don't look so worried. Remember, you can keep taking this test."

"If you say so, Methuselah," I muttered to myself. I started to walk back to my seat.

"Glena Davies," Kathy called out. "Someone just called asked for you and hung up."

I froze mid-stride.

"It was a lady's voice," she said.

"Oh, oh. Thank you," I replied.

I was hyperventilating and feeling light-headed. I ran outside to my car, but I couldn't find it. I walked up and down the block a few times—still no car.

Jerome saw me and asked what was wrong. When I told him, he offered to drive me to look for it. About the third time around the block, he said, "Maybe you got towed."

Then I remembered that because I had arrived so early that day, I had parked for the first time at the back of the Kaplan lot. After dropping me off, I thanked him and then drove jubilantly back to Pewaukee.

THE MATCH GAME

Doris was holding Sean and the open letter. "It's an 82, an 82. Tell Mommy. We got her 82!"

I was on an adrenaline high. It was a happy day—I was too happy to eat, drink, or sleep. I called everyone. Doris even let me phone my sister Olive long distance.

I called Elaine and told her the news. She was thrilled. "When you come to pick up Sean on Friday, the staff and I want to take you to the Old Country Buffet.

"Thank you," I replied breathlessly.

Doris was proud and happy for me, and I asked her to field all the calls that came in from church members who had phoned to congratulate me.

I took Sean and went for a walk. There was a serious discussion I needed to have with God.

"Okay, God," I began. "I'm so sorry I doubted You." On and on I went, throwing kisses in the air, alternately weeping and laughing. The cold air was refreshing. My light-headedness was replaced with lightheartedness. I was back on the bus with God, all the wheels turning.

The next day at Kaplan, Kathy chided me. "You didn't turn in your modules yesterday. You know the rules."

I apologized. "I guess I was too overjoyed about my results."

"What? You passed?" she asked.

"Yes," I answered, excitedly.

Then she said, "You look different today."

I just smiled. While I had let my hair mound on my head like tired coils of an old mattress, overnight I had washed and cut my hair, and gotten rid of my wool hat. It was a new day, a new beginning.

I later learned that no one else in our study group had passed the Preclinical exam.

More Than Lemon Drops

On Sundays after church I would go to the Waukesha Hospital library. On the librarian's desk sat a small bowl of lemon drops. No matter how many I took out of the bowl, I would find it full whenever I returned. I usually took more than I should, making it my snack for the day.

The Clinical Modules at Kaplan were easier, and I got through them faster, allowing me to spend more time at the hospital library. One afternoon Linda, the librarian, approached me and said, "I have a friend who is an ear, nose, and throat specialist at Waukesha Memorial Hospital, and he mentioned that a small group of hospital interns have a noon conference every day. You should join them."

Phew! I thought it was about the lemon drops!

She took me over to meet her friend, and he introduced me to the chief resident, Paul. When he heard my background, I was welcomed into the group.

Paul shared the routine. "We usually get lunch in the cafeteria and bring it to the conference." That's what I did, and for a couple of dollars, I had a delicious tray of food. It became my main meal of the day.

During this time tragedy struck at the Steele household. Doris suffered a massive stroke and died on the front lawn of the farmhouse. Ken was devastated, and so was I. Even though I continued to live there, I made sure that my daily routine did not place a hardship on Ken in any way. I thanked God for those cafeteria meals each day.

At the noon conferences, I met interns and residents from various specialties. And while the Clinical Modules at Kaplan were accurate, they were not as up-to-date as those noon clinical conferences.

Paul began coaching me on how the system worked and the steps I needed to take. He also brought to my attention a directory listing all the hospitals in the United States. I wrote down the address of about fifty medical centers—each of them in the eastern half of the country, because it was the only area I was even slightly familiar with.

Paul explained that I should be flexible regarding my future specialty. "Not every hospital may have a slot for what you are seeking." Until then, I had my heart set on OB/GYN, but my experience with children in Zorzor also had me thinking about pediatrics.

I bought a box of envelopes and while I was at the library, I began writing letters, describing my background and what specialty of medicine I was interested in.

Linda came over to me and asked, "Glena, what are you doing?"

When I explained, she smiled and responded, "I think I can save you a lot of time."

The next thing I knew, she had beautifully typed my letter on a computer program, inserted the names and addresses of the recipients, merged the files and printed the envelopes. Wow! I couldn't believe how professional the finished products looked.

Some were directed to the Department of Obstetrics and Gynecology, others to the Department of Pediatrics, and a few to the Department of Family Medicine. The goal was just to get my foot in the door.

That night I fell to my knees and prayed, "God, please forgive me for doubting You. My glasses were foggy, but I'm beginning to see a lot more clearly now."

If the embers began to show signs of dying down, I pressed on those bellows until the fire roared once more. I could make it on four hours of sleep at night and one meal a day. There was no holding me back; it was as if my brain chemistry had changed and I was charging full-speed ahead. Even though I knew none of the residency programs would accept me until they had all my scores and I had passed the second part of the ECFMG test, the letters were to let them know I was out there and to initiate some communication with them.

Was I a Sixth Finger?

Then reality slapped me in the face. Since Doris Steele had died, I knew that Sean and I should not continue to live at Ken's house. I felt it was too much of a burden on him.

I was fearful, though, because I had no place to go, very little money, and practically no clothes to speak of. I began to imagine myself as a sixth finger—always attached to something, always needing food and water, but with absolutely no purpose. My mind drifted back to my childhood in Freetown. I was the third but unnecessary daughter. What did my parents need—yet another mouth to feed? They had wanted a son. It seemed I was still rowing that same boat.

My sister Olive had emigrated to the United States and was living in Virginia with her husband and child. I contacted her, saying, "I don't know what your situation is, but could Sean and I come and stay in your basement for a while?"

There was a Kaplan Test Prep center nearby where I could continue studying for the clinical medical exam. This didn't work out, but Olive was aware of my plight and mailed me some of her old clothes. It reminded me once again of life on Waterloo Street. I settled back into my routine of studying.

Not long after, I took the clinical component of the ECFMG exam without emotional gyrations, and I passed. It was time to navigate the system. I now had to apply to residency programs, prepare to be interviewed . . . and wait.

One morning, Pat Kern called me and asked if I would accompany her to the nearby shopping mall. "I have a hard time with the buttons and hooks when I try on clothes, and you could really help me."

While we were there, one of the attendants pulled me over to a rack of dresses and said, "You would really look good in some of these. Would you like to try them on?"

Knowing my situation, I cordially answered, "Thank you, but I'm not shopping today."

Mrs. Kern, overhearing, jumped in, saying, "Oh, go ahead, Glena. It will be fun to see how you look in a few of them." So, to make her happy, I complied. The clothes really made me look good.

After about an hour, the attendant brought out a large garment bag and Pat asked me, "Would you help me and carry this to the car?"

On the drive back to the Steele's house, she thanked me for helping her and kept saying what a wonderful shopping day it had been.

Then she popped open the trunk and said, "Glena, I want you to take the garment bag inside."

At that moment I realized I had been duped. I unzipped a portion of the bag and saw that every suit I had tried on was inside. Pat had not purchased a single outfit for herself. She thought I could use proper clothes for any upcoming interviews.

I staggered into the house. It was one of those times when it was as if God was right in my face, reminding me, "I told you I would take care of you. Why do you have so much doubt, fear, and worry?"

I treasured those beautiful clothes for years and years.

The "Match"

During my lunchtime with the interns in Waukesha, I learned about the National Resident Matching Program, which is a *must* for medical residency placement. It is an algorithm program. You submit your data to them along with a list of all the hospitals you have applied to. After mailing the letters, you patiently wait for a response from the hospitals on your list. Hopefully you receive a reply that shows their interest and an invitation for an interview at a particular date.

After your visit, the "Match" sends you a form on which you are to rank your preference for that hospital from one to however many you applied to. The residency program fills out a similar form—ranking you as a potential candidate for them.

As part of the contract, which all parties sign, a potential candidate cannot join any residency outside the match without severe penalties. And similarly, no residency program can accept a candidate outside of the match program without penalty.

The wait to hear from the hospitals I had applied to seemed to stretch on forever. Match day in America is always in March. Winter in Wisconsin was long. Waiting was so hard, and March seemed so far away.

I was literally running on fumes—not just on gas for my car, but in my heart. Doubts began to flood my mind once more: *What if I am interviewed by these residency programs and none of them take me?* My student visa would expire in July, just in time to start residency. But first I had to get in.

The war in Liberia raged on. Sierra Leone was in shambles. The official civil war was not recognized and declared until 1991 when Charles Taylor's National Patriotic Front of Liberia helped the Revolutionary United Front in Sierra Leone, in an attempt to overthrow Joseph Momoh's government.

I had nowhere to run, nowhere to hide.

The Interviews

After what seemed like an eternity, I finally received my first invitation for an interview. It was from the OB/GYN department at the Ohio State University. This was followed by interviews at the hospital in Waukesha—one in Family Medicine and the second in Pediatrics.

I really got excited when I received an invitation from the residency program at Ohio State Medical Center in Columbus. I knew the area well since I had received my Masters at OSU.

The news caused a buzz of excitement among my church friends. However, when Bob Kern heard that I planned to drive to Columbus, Ohio, he got in touch with me, asking, "You're not going to drive that green Oldsmobile over there, are you?"

That had been my plan. In fact I had already phoned my friend Bill Guthrie and his wife in Ohio, asking them if they could take care of Sean while I was there. They were delighted. It was Bill who taught at Wilmington College where I finished my undergraduate degree.

Bob Kern called me again. "Glena, our firm has a number of company cars. We're having one tuned up that you can use on your visits to hospitals out of state."

This news was a godsend.

The next invitation arrived from a major hospital in Miami, Florida. They expressed interest in me because of my background in tropical medicine in Africa.

It would be a lengthy road trip, and I planned to take Sean along.

Once more Bob Kern stepped in. "It's a long way to Florida," he told me. "Are you sure you want to drive?"

A couple of days later, I received a call from Bob's secretary: "Mr. Kern knows you are planning on going to Miami. He has an envelope for a friend there, and he would like you to take it with you."

At the office she asked me to open the envelope—and inside was a round trip airline ticket to Miami. I could take Sean, since he was young enough to fly free.

The Kerns were extremely generous, yet they never took my dignity away—and they never requested anything of me in return. They were always in the background, and if they saw I needed help, they stepped in to fill the gap.

In the letter of invitation from Miami, it said, "Feel free to bring your significant other."

I thanked them and told them I would.

I took my son. The hospital had a daycare center, where I enrolled him for each day of the two-day visit. One of the administrators said, "I thought you were bringing your significant other."

I replied, "I did. He's in your nursery." I wanted them to know that I was a single mom.

During my exit interview in Miami, an administrator got right to the point and shocked me by saying, "We really like you. Can you start tomorrow?"

I was blown away!

How could they make such an offer? It would be violating the rules of the Match program—which we both had signed. This was a real dilemma since an hour earlier I had nowhere to go, and now I was being offered a future. It was the first indication that anyone really wanted me in a program.

However, the thought of breaking the rules upset my stomach, and I said, "I can't do this."

When I returned to Waukesha and told Linda at the library what had happened, she reassured me. "You made the right decision. That program must really be in bad shape if they don't have enough people to fill the positions," she said. "And what does that say about their integrity?"

I let the hospital in Miami know that if I did not receive a residency position under the Match Program, and was no longer under contract, perhaps we could talk again. I wasn't about to close any doors.

An Unexpected Letter

One of the interns in Waukesha introduced me to a private practice family medicine doctor who also taught at the medical college. His clinic was in Delafield, Wisconsin, about twenty minutes from Waukesha. "You can come to my clinic to sharpen your history and physical skills. Could you be there two days a week and take care of writing up the histories and physicals of my patients?" he asked.

His practice was a very busy one. Soon I was wearing a borrowed white coat, and I blended in with other residents who showed up.

I was hesitant at first, and I told him that I really didn't have the money for gas to get back and forth. "Would twenty dollars a week help?" he asked.

Once I stopped studying at Kaplan, I no longer drove to Milwaukee or to the Catholic relief agency. This was my new lifeline. I was earning it, and I felt better.

Then came an unexpected letter that was addressed to me at the Steele's address. I was developing an unrealistic fear of mailboxes and opening envelopes. As I held the letter, I was filled with a strong sense of foreboding. Letters change lives.

With fear and trepidation, I looked at the return address. It was from a United Nations box number.

Slowly I opened the envelope, and there was a one-sentence, cryptic note: "Glena, expect a phone call from me. John."

That was it. Nothing more. My aversion to letters, telegrams, mailboxes, and envelopes was strengthened. Evidently one of the many letters I had sent via the United Nations must have reached him.

My heart didn't just skip a beat, it was racing faster than a high-speed train. I wondered, *What is he about to tell me? Is my life about to drastically change?*

Three days later the phone rang. It was John. "Glena, can you hear me?" he began.

"Yes," I answered softly. I could hardly speak because I was so emotional and close to tears.

His next words were a dagger to my heart. "I am so sad and sorry for everything. I am trying to help Bernice. We are now back together. I don't know how to help you."

I grew deathly quiet. It was as if someone was reading a prepared script.

Then he added, "I am calling from an officers' club and really can't talk long."

My mind was speeding a hundred miles an hour with all the things I wanted to tell him. I did let him know that Sean was a beautiful child, that I had passed the ECMFG test, and was doing my utmost to get into a residency program.

His only comment was, "Well, you are very bright, and I know things will work out just fine for you."

Had he said, "But you have medicine," I would have died right on the spot.

And that was it. No further explanation, no words of comfort. Nothing.

For the next few days I rehearsed in my mind all that had taken place. John had been my knight in shining armor who rescued me from a disastrous marriage. I also knew that Sean was born out of pure love. But now all hope for a future with John was gone. I was truly on my own and had to focus on the immediate. It was back to Sierra Leone and almost certain death, or life in the United States with an unknown future. It was obvious that I could only depend on God and myself.

There were days when it seemed that cynicism and anger were my brothers—with each sitting on separate shoulders. One would chide, "I told you so," and the other, "Do you think you have a right to happiness like everybody else?"

Anxious Days

Now for the nail-biting. Would I be a match for one of the hospitals where I had interviewed? There were seven, including Penn State Hershey Medical Center in Pennsylvania.

My anxious days fell into a routine of helping out at the clinic in Delafield, picking up Sean, and eating one meal a day. The noon conferences with interns had ended. I became rather fatalistic concerning my future, telling myself, "If I don't get into a residency, it must be God's way of letting me know it's over."

Four things really bothered me. First, I was well aware that American-trained medical students had a huge advantage over foreign graduates. Second, John had disappeared from the picture.

Third, I didn't have U.S. citizenship, so it would be practically impossible for me to get a job in the States. Fourth, the war in Liberia was beginning to spill over into Sierra Leone, so that door was slowly closing.

Once more, desperation was beginning to set in, and my confidence in the future was shaky.

Would My Number Be There?

I received a letter from the National Resident Matching Program, announcing the specific schedule for Match Day—and assigning a four-digit personal identity number (PIN) to me.

On a preannounced date, the numbers (not the names) of the students who had "matched" were posted in *USA Today.*

If your number wasn't there—well, I didn't even want to think about that scenario!

The following day, those who matched would receive a certified letter telling them the name of the hospital where they would do their residency.

When I received my number, I was so excited that I told everybody, "Write it down. And next Wednesday find a rack where they sell *USA Today* and get a copy. If my number is there, please call me."

I knew the paper was distributed in our area about 6:00 a.m., but I didn't have the nerve to buy a copy and see the results myself.

Early that morning, before the sun came up, I drove to the cemetery where Doris Steele was buried. This was the woman I had come to call "Mom." At her grave I said out loud, "Doris, you know this has been a hard road. If I am laid to rest here, I take pleasure in the fact that I am near someone I love and who knows what I have been through. Perhaps everything I have worked for will be for naught."

I was determined not to go out in silence. If I was going to die, it would have to be right here with the people who had shown me so much compassion.

Then I drove back to the house.

The Day Everything Changed

I knew I would receive at least one phone call that morning since I told Frank and Marylou, "If you don't find my match number in the paper, just ring me anyway and let me know."

At a quarter past six the phone rang. When I picked it up, the voice on the other end was hysterical, screaming, "Glena, you made it! You made it!" It was David Marose, Frank and Marylou's son.

For the next hour I received one call after another, with the most excited voices you can imagine. But no one was more thrilled than me!

I was on my way—to who knew where! Awaiting me would be a real job with a salary, subsidized housing, meals at the cafeteria, and health care for my son and me. The people in the church rejoiced with me.

Elaine from the day care called and wanted to take us to the Old Country Buffet to celebrate. What a joy to know that I would finally be able to pay her back for the trust she had placed in me and the love and kindness she had shown to Sean.

That was the day everything in my life changed for the better.

The next afternoon, I was standing on the edge of the highway, near the mailbox, waiting for the letter. Would it be Ohio State? The University of Wisconsin? Where? And what would my medical specialty be?

After a while Ken called me to the house. "Here," he said, "this mail arrived early for you. I think it's the letter you've been looking for."

It was from Pennsylvania State University. I ripped into the envelope and it read, "Dear Dr. Glena Davies, we are delighted that you will be joining us at our hospital in Hershey in the pediatric program."

I was wide open and receptive to whatever God had in store for me, but now it was settled. I was going to be a pediatrician!

CHAPTER SIXTEEN

HERSHEY—IT WASN'T ALL KISSES

As I held the letter from Hershey in my hand, it suddenly occurred to me that the blueprint I had demanded that God produce when things seemed impossibly difficult had been there all along.

I started to laugh. It was like finally getting to see the front side of a woven tapestry—instead of its knotted backside, which only hints at possibilities, with no clarity.

Zorzor! It was all so clear now.

I had been miffed at the male patients who obviously made their preferences for being seen by a male colleague known. I had complained loudly to nurses about seeing mostly women and children on "big clinic days."

"Look," I protested, "he and I were in the same class. They trained us both equally—women and men!" But week after week it was the same. I was seeing mostly women with their children, and only a few men and boys.

Finally an old man whose complaints included headaches, urinary frequency, and mild incontinence set me straight. The nurse had just handed me his negative urine screen for sugar. I pulled the privacy screen to check his prostate for enlargement. "Unh-uh, doctor," he protested. "I told you my head hurt, not my butt!"

He stormed over to my male colleague's side of the clinic.

My blinders were on so tightly that I could not see the long line of women and children who waited patiently each week to lay the template for what would become my life's work.

Now, as I was about to enter my U.S. residency, I shook my head and chided myself for my shortsightedness. "You asked Me for a blueprint. I gave it to You," I heard God say.

Yes, I was having a chat with God again.

Car Trouble?

Match Day had come and gone. I was readying myself to begin the residency July 1, 1988, in Hershey, Pennsylvania. I returned the borrowed car to the Kerns and spent the rest of the spring and early summer helping out at the clinic in Delafield—driving back and forth in my green fender-bender.

When I received the package from Penn State with the details of what I could expect on my arrival, I decided to make a quick trip to Hershey to meet the administrators, check out housing, day care, and so on. When I arrived, the director of resident affairs gave me a warm welcome.

The interim pastor of our church, Susan, had volunteered to take care of Sean while I was gone. When I returned, the people in our congregation threw a combined birthday and going away party for us, with presents and toys for Sean, who turned three on May 7. Many handed me envelopes with personal notes inside, and some included a twenty dollar bill or a small cheque. I was overwhelmed.

A couple of weeks before Sean and I were to leave for Hershey, I looked at my son's crib and all his new toys and thought, *I sure hope these will fit in my jalopy.* My goal was to drive the "green bomb" there and trade it in for something better as soon as I had a couple of paychecks in the bank.

Bob and Pat Kern were always in the background, whether I knew it or not. Pat had asked me and Sean to call her "Grandma." It was fitting—she had been so loving and kind to Sean. Around that time there was a phone call from Pat. She asked if I could come over to their house. "Grandpa needs your help," she told me. "He will be outside, so just park next to the car."

When I arrived I saw a blue automobile with the hood up. I assumed he was having engine trouble. However, his first question to me didn't seem to make sense.

"If you have any personal items in your car, just put them in the back seat of this one." I didn't have much with me, except for one of Sean's blankets.

Then he said, "Sit in the driver's seat. When I tell you to pump the accelerator, do it." I did. Then he asked me to stop and start the engine a couple of times.

Next he instructed me to put the car in "drive" and pull out of the driveway. Then I heard him yell, "When you get home, call me!"

I figured something was fishy. When I called him, Bob told me, "The car is yours. It's one of our company vehicles that has a lot of miles on it, but I had Frank Marose tune it up, and it should get you to Hershey just fine." It was a four-door Ford.

It reminded me of the day I went to Joanne and Larry's to pick up Sean. They had been watching him all day, and when I arrived, there they were in their backyard, laughing heartily, with Sean squealing in a swing set they had bought and erected for him. Their children were already adults, and they didn't have any grandchildren.

I have been blessed to be the recipient of many gifts, and I instinctively know the difference between those who give wanting something in return and those whose generosity flows from a heart of love. The congregation at First Baptist was always in the second category.

Child Scare

Settling into my residency at the hospital took a little time, but the people were warm and welcoming. When I received my first paycheck, although it wasn't huge, I felt like a millionaire.

With a great sense of satisfaction and accomplishment, I was able to send a cheque to Elaine at the day care center in Wisconsin to repay her for the faith and trust she had placed in me.

My biggest challenge in Hershey was finding a child care facility for Sean while I was working at the hospital—a necessity others in the program weren't burdened with.

About a week after I enrolled my son at a recommended child care facility, I arrived twenty minutes early to pick him up. What I found was very disturbing. I looked through the window into the room where Sean and a group of youngsters were sitting on a rug. Then I noticed that one toddler, clearly unwell, was alone in another room, covered with vomit and stool.

There was no adult in either room, and I could have easily picked up any child and walked out the door. I called out loud many times before I found a worker.

Needless to say, I immediately pulled him out of that center, and I found a woman who offered day care in her home. Unfortunately that didn't work out either. One day when I arrived to pick Sean up, the care giver was out cold on the sofa, not just sleeping, but *snoring*!

Instead of waking her up, I suppressed my anger, picked up Sean, and left. I did not leave a note.

About an hour later, I received an urgent phone call from the concerned woman. "Can you come over right now? I need your help." I knew the reason why—she couldn't find Sean! I told her what I had done, and that was strikeout number two on the child care search.

Without the supportive network the church had provided, balancing Sean's care with a hectic residency training proved exceedingly difficult. I aired my concerns to my advisor. He agreed but offered no solutions.

Family Dynamics

Back in Sierra Leone, there was more political unrest, and the war that began in Liberia had spilled across the border. The military was looking for able-bodied young men to fight on behalf of the government. Reports were circulating about how the rebels would capture young men and order them to shoot their own mothers. It was an initiation test—and if you passed they knew you would kill on command. Obeying was the only way you could receive your food rations.

I immediately began worrying about my brother, Ian. He was in his early twenties and healthy, so I thought, *I can kill two birds with one stone. If I can bring him to America, he can help take care of Sean and also study for his Graduate Record Examination (GRE)*. Ian had finished his undergraduate degree in agriculture and was ready to start a master's program. With the country in shambles, this might be a solution that would benefit all three of us: me, Ian, and Sean.

I went to the bank and applied for a loan—enough for his plane ticket and his living expenses for a short period. I used my car as collateral. The bank approved the loan, and Ian came to stay in my two-room apartment.

Sean was now an active four-year-old and was enrolled in a preschool. Ian seemed to be adjusting well to life in America.

Part of my residency training included working at an outpatient clinic. The critiques provided by the mentors were invaluable.

One day the residency director entered the room unexpectedly, pulled me aside, and said, "Glena, we need to speak to you privately."

In the hallway were two uniformed police. I could tell something was seriously wrong. They asked, "Do you have a telephone at your house?" I was baffled. I answered affirmatively. Then they pulled out a printout from the phone company—and it all started to ring a bell.

A few weeks earlier I had gone to the business office to complain because the bill I received for one month was over eight hundred dollars, and I knew there had to be some mistake. "Look," I told them, "the same number is being dialed over and over again. I'm sure there is a computer glitch." And some of the calls lasted for more than an hour.

They promised, "We will look into the matter and let you know."

The phone company got back to me all right—by sending two policemen to the clinic in full view of my colleagues! They showed me a new bill that was for an additional four hundred dollars.

"Tell me the truth. Did you make these calls?" one officer inquired.

"No, sir," I answered. When he repeated the question, I replied, "As God is my witness, I did not make those calls."

Without my knowledge the phone company had requested a court order allowing them to actually listen to some of those calls, and they heard a man and woman conversing on the line. They even knew the woman's name. So they already knew it wasn't me, but they were trying to see if I was deliberately misleading them. They were concerned that some fraud was being perpetrated.

"Tell me the number of people residing in your house," they said.

"It's just me and my four-year-old son," I answered. But after a few moments I remembered that Ian had been with me for about six months. "And, oh yes, my brother is visiting."

Then I added, "It couldn't be my brother making those calls—he doesn't know anybody in this country. If you'll wait a minute, I will phone him."

And I did. When I reached Ian, I asked, "Do you know this number?" I read it to him.

"Oh yes," he answered without hesitating. "That's my girlfriend." And he hung up.

At that moment, all the blood drained from my head and down to my feet. I felt woozy. I told the officers, "He is at my apartment right now. You can go and talk to him." I called Ian back and let him know that some policemen were on their way over to talk to him.

I told the officers that he had just arrived from Africa and likely didn't know or realize the cost of long distance calls. He was isolated in the apartment. Sean was gone all morning, and I was gone practically all the time, and when I did come home, it was to cook, clean, and sleep. Though he had been rescued out of a potentially life-threatening situation in Sierra Leone, life as he knew it had come to a screeching halt. He was looking for companionship.

I reassured the officers that no collusion was intended. This way they could determine for themselves that I was not trying to defraud the system. I had no idea he had found friends.

It took quite a while, but we finally solved the issue with the phone company, clearing our good name.

The Turmoil

The winter was busy. My rotation was in the hospital ICU, and there was so much to learn in so little time.

One day my emergency pager buzzed. I went to a phone, and the operator connected me with my neighbor who lived downstairs at our apartment building. He said, "I hate to bother you, but your son is alone outside. He keeps banging on your door, yelling, 'Uncle, let me in.' I tried to bring him to our house because it's so cold, but he told me that his mommy warned him that he shouldn't talk to strangers."

I literally ran out of the ICU—which was against the rules—and rescued Sean. I brought him back to the hospital and called an off-duty resident friend, explaining, "I need your help." She came right over and took care of Sean for a couple of hours until I got off work.

It was a difficult evening to get through when Ian returned home later. He had instructed Sean to go to a friend's house after school (which was in the same quadrangle as our apartment), but Sean forgot. After all, he was only four years old.

Ian wasn't with us long. He had developed friendships of his own and was planning to marry an American girl. He also was being recruited to join the U.S. Army. He did not share any of these plans with me.

It must have been incredibly difficult for him to simply stand by and watch my life take form while his seemingly had screeched to a halt. He too had faced and crossed the ocean and was navigating his own journey. We were both stuck on this side of the Atlantic. Different views of our situation was now the center of family discussions.

My view was simple. My training would end in two short years. In exchange for his care of Sean, I would support Ian through graduate or professional school once I was gainfully employed.

Our siblings weighed in. "He is not your babysitter," one said. The family was imploding.

Residency was difficult, but we were given alternate weekends off. It afforded residents time to read journals, regroup with family, and rest—and prepare papers for noon presentations on the wards.

Every other weekend Ian, Sean, and I would travel to my sister Olive's house in Virginia. Ian would drive while I slept in the back seat. We would eat the food I brought while Leslie, Olive's son, entertained and played with Sean so Ian could get a break. Soon this arrangement began to fray. Ian had Army recuiters to talk to and friends to see. Olive could not negotiate the freeway to drive to Hershey, and I was too sleep-deprived to negotiate the trip to Virginia.

The news from Sierra Leone was grave. More and more I came to realize that while the pursuit of my profession and parenting were not incompatible, it was ultimately going to be my Achilles' heel. My second year of residency was ending and evaluations were pending.

One of the evaluators wrote, "Glena, you are not doing badly, but you are certainly not performing at the level you are capable of."

I knew they were right. After some discussion, we mutually agreed to a three-month extension of my rotations while I sorted out my family life.

My Mother at Risk

My friends in Monrovia at the Lutheran Compound sent word to me that the war in Sierra Leone was inching closer and closer to Freetown. I learned that nine- and ten-year-old kids were taking up arms. They were wild and hungry, being controlled with marijuana and cocaine. Some were even told, "If you want to eat, go to a house and kill everyone there and then eat their rice and chicken."

It seemed that people were bent on sharing only bad news of Sierra Leone and Liberia with me. It wasn't their fault; there was nothing good to report. One of my mom's elderly well-to-do neighbors was murdered by the young rebels. The reports said that there wasn't an inch on her body that didn't have stab wounds. They also raided her house of every belonging.

By this time 38 Waterloo Street was now a different place. Both my sisters had married and left home. Olive lived in Virginia, and Gloria in London. Ian had lived with me in Hershey until his marriage to Lisa; they now lived in Williamsport, Pennsylvania.

During my second year of medical school, Grandma Constance had died at age eighty-four. She had lived long enough to see me get married and had presided over the chicken pepper soup that is customarily made for the bride on her wedding day to share with the bride's oldest living female relative. We had eaten the soup together, through both tears and laughter.

At Constance's funeral, it was standing room only. People complained that all the boats available to ferry between Bonthe and Freetown were filled to capacity with people on their way to attend her funeral. While everyone jubilantly celebrated her life, I alone cried. I had lost my greatest fan.

I knew that my mother was at severe risk, so I wrote to my siblings. "We must get her out of there. If she comes to live with me, I can take care of her, and she can help take care of Sean."

Back to the loan officer at the bank I went. Now I was in my third year of residency and had established a good track record with them, so they advanced the funds I needed. Olive had become a U.S. citizen, and she arranged Sisi's travel visa.

I was overjoyed when Sisi arrived in 1990, although I must say that the culture shock and isolation was traumatic for her. It was not unlike transplanting a full-grown tree. Small seedlings fared so much better—and Sisi was no seedling! She struggled with every aspect of life in America. The food was not spicy enough; the weather was too cold. "I am a refugee here," she would wail.

Everyone who had crossed the Atlantic felt the residual turbulence of their journey; no one seemed immune. I became sad—she became depressed.

My Decision—or Sean's?

Midway through my final year of residency, things really turned around for me. My evaluations had improved. I had taken and passed the federal licencing exam and was looking for final approval to become a full-fledged, certified medical doctor with U.S. credentials. I only had the Pediatric Board Certifying Exam left to take.

During the final year, the records of every resident doctor across the nation are entered into a data bank. This information is available to every hospital, clinic, and health organization in America. Those who need your services for their staffing would contact you.

One of the first letters I opened was from an organization called New Physicians for Wisconsin. Their purpose was to help address health needs, especially in areas that were underserved. This was appealing since I had so many friends in Wisconsin.

I also received an invitation to interview with the Centers for Disease Control and Prevention (CDC) in Atlanta, the leading national health institute in the U.S. They especially wanted me to come for a face-to-face meeting because of my interest in childhood infectious diseases. My time in Zorzor had really helped. Almost simultaneously I was invited to interview with Emory University.

So I flew to Atlanta.

By the time I flew back to Hershey, Emory had called, extending an invitation to sign with them and start immediately in the specialty of pediatric infectious diseases. Sean was now six years old and becoming quite an expressive conversationalist. When he saw how excited I was about the possibility of going to work in Atlanta, he asked, "Mommy, will you have to spend any nights at the hospital?"

"Well, some nights I may have to," I answered.

Immediately he threw himself down on the floor and began to sob; he could hardly stop. Then with a very sad face he said, "Mommy, I never want you to leave me again."

A few days later we were at a shopping mall when he suddenly fell to the floor and started crying uncontrollably. Not knowing what was bothering him, I scooped him up and carried him to the car. When he finally calmed down, I asked, "What's wrong?"

"Didn't you see that?" he asked.

"What are you talking about?"

"That man . . . he was carrying his boy on his shoulders."

Then he uttered words that tore at my heart. "I don't have a daddy like that."

It was at that moment I decided that I would not be going to Atlanta, or any other hospital. The situation in Wisconsin looked more and more appealing. I could set up my own practice, and Sean and I would never have to be separated.

That Mailbox Phobia

I knew there was an exciting future out there with my name on it, but once again life's shenanigans arose to terrify me.

My mother often got the mail, but one day I stopped at the

mailbox. There was a letter from the U.S. Immigration Services. When I opened it, I could hardly believe what I read. On blue paper, in large letters at the top of the page were printed these words: DEPORTATION ORDER.

Under this was a notice saying there was a lapse in my visa renewal and I had to leave the country by the date written on the order.

This made no sense. After all, to even be admitted to a residency program, I had to apply for what is called a "J-1 visa," a non-immigrant visa issued by the United States to research scholars, professors, and exchange visitors participating in various programs, including receiving medical training within the U.S.

I made sure that all the legal paperwork regarding my stay in the U.S. would be handled by an attorney. I found one in Milwaukee who had been highly recommended. His name was Harold Block. He requested one hundred dollars to process the documents, which I sent him by certified mail. Then, each January I would have the visa renewed by sending him another hundred dollars for him to keep everything current.

Confused about the deportation order, I immediately called the attorney's office for some answers. His secretary said, "I'll give him the message, and I'm sure he will call you back shortly."

I heard nothing from him, even though I called with the same request day after day. I knew that Mr. Block used to be a pharmacist before going into law. In fact he now owned a pharmacy business near the area where I had lived. My old friend, Kathy Hawley, had become a pharmacist and now worked at his pharmacy. So I called her, saying, "I know Mr. Block stops by the drug store every night to check on the business. Would you ask him about this matter and tell him I am waiting for a response?"

A couple of days later, she called me. "Glena, something is odd. Every time I bring up the matter, he just shrugs his shoulders. Do you owe him money?"

I let her know that every year I sent him money to take care of my visa renewal, and I had the return certified receipts from the post office as proof. I called the attorney's secretary for the umpteenth time and, running out of patience, demanded, "I will not hang up this phone until I talk to Mr. Block." By my tone she knew I meant business and put him directly on the line.

He told me, "I'm sorry, but we can't find the paperwork."

"Don't Say a Word"

Not knowing what to do, I placed a call to Bob Kern. It was rare that I had ever called him directly to make a request of him, but I was desperate. When I explained my dire predicament, that I was about to be deported, he immediately drove over to Harold Block's office and said, "I am here on behalf of Glena Davies," and demanded answers.

Mr. Kern called me back and said, "The attorney told me that he thought your paperwork was misplaced in a closed file, and he didn't have it anymore."

What was I to do? The New Physicians for Wisconsin had asked me to forward certain documents to their office. I called them and said, "If you send me a list of everything you need, I'll put it into one file and mail it to you." It was really a delaying tactic on my part, knowing my visa wasn't in order.

Bob Kern walked out of Harold Block's office totally upset. He hired an attorney, Mary Stevenson, that same day. She had worked for the Immigration and Naturalization Service at one time and knew the ropes.

This new lawyer called me, introduced herself, and said, "Glena, starting this very moment, do not fill out any paperwork for anybody, and don't go to any interviews until you talk with me personally."

Bob Kern arranged for me to fly to Milwaukee for a day to meet the new attorney. Before the flight, she called me and said, "Don't tell anyone where you are going. Just come straight to my office."

When I returned to Hershey, there were several calls from the CDC and other hospitals waiting for my reply—and an urgent request from the program in Wisconsin to mail the documents they needed. But I followed Mary Stevenson's advice and kept silent.

Mary was like a bulldog on the visa issue. She filed a lawsuit against Harold Block—charging negligence resulting in the deportation order. She also arranged an emergency hearing before the Supreme Court of the State of Wisconsin—one that didn't require me to appear in person. She handled it all.

It finally came down to the fact that, through no fault of my own, I was out of visa status, and the only way to be legal was to physically leave the country and enter it again with a brand new visa. Mary took care of a mountain of paperwork that would make this happen. She told me, "You and Sean will fly to Barbados for ten days. While there, you will go over to the U.S. Embassy. They know all about this case and will give you a new V-1 visa along with documents to show the customs officials when you reenter the country through Puerto Rico."

Barbados! What a wonderful "vacation" . . . if you could call it that. I was on pins and needles the whole time.

Coming back into the U.S. went like clockwork, and I was now once again legal. Mary even called the New Physicians for Wisconsin officials to let them know that she was acting on my behalf and all the paperwork would be in order.

In my scrapbook is a news clipping from the *Waukesha Freeman* newspaper with a headline reading, "Doctor Sues Lawyer and Wins."

The Checklist Miracle

There was one more river to cross.

The exit interview, which every resident had to undergo, included a checklist ensuring that every obligation had been met. As a non-citizen entering the residency program, I had to show proof of an appropriate visa that met the requirements of employment. My application and yearly renewal of the visa fulfilled that requirement.

The J-1 visa has a "Mandatory Repatriation" clause which, of course, I had signed at the start of residency. To the best of my knowledge, Harold Block had renewed it annually and sent me a receipt for the renewal fee via certified mail as I had required of him.

During the exit interview, I sat stiffly next to our Director of Residency Affairs, May Wallace, and across from the human resources personnel. We started going down the checklist:

All patient charts completed, dictated, and signed? May looked at her list and checked the "Yes" box.

All out-patients informed via letter on Penn State letterhead of completion of program? "Yes."

Outstanding utility bills? "None."

HR cross-checked the maintenance department's list. No problems found? May checked the "Yes" box.

Then on to "Other." Visa requirements.

How was I going to answer about the Mandatory Repatriation requirement under the J-1 visa? Technically, I didn't then, or *ever,* have a J-1 visa. I was in the country legally with the help of my new attorney, but not with a J-1 visa.

I was frozen and felt nauseous. Until the deportation notice, I believed that I had a J-1 visa. How was I going to answer? Over the years, as soon as I received the certified mail back from Harold Block, I would make a xerox copy of the receipts to give to May Wallace. Here they were, now next to May's folder.

I wondered, *Should I stop the interview and tell them what I know before they ask me anything?*

I dropped my head, fearing that the contents of my stomach would soon land all over the table. I felt very queasy. Then I remembered what the attorney had told me: "Answer truthfully, but only to questions you are asked."

May Wallace rifled through the papers, pulled back her chair, and said, "We are done here." She congratulated me, saying, "You've worked so diligently. You keep in touch." As she hugged me goodbye, she had no idea why I was crying so hard.

Months later, I passed the Pediatric Board Examination and became a board-certified pediatrician.

Technical incidents, which at the time seemed like death sentences, turned out to be life-saving miracles. Call it what you will—God was in my corner.

By this time, the U.S. Department of Justice and other organizations such as Amnesty International had documented the numerous atrocities that were happening in Sierra Leone. They had evidence of my detention at the Lungi airport, Sean being taken by the flight attendants, and the detour to Amsterdam where the Netherlands custom officials documented details before I was allowed to board for the flight to the U.S.

When my case was presented to the Immigration and Naturalization Service (INS), my attorney was able to show that it wasn't a simple case of bribery when I was being hassled about the hundred-dollar bill found in my pocket. This was the pretense used to identify persons suspected to have been "friends of America" with covert anti-Sierra Leone and Liberian sentiments. Moreover, I was a friend of Ellen Johnson Sirleaf, now in rebel custody.

They had evidence of several individuals who had been identified in this way and, when detained and returned to Freetown, were never seen or heard from again. My lawyer said that this demonstrated clear evidence of danger to my life should I be required to return to Sierra Leone.

For the present moment, while the war was in full bloom, the mandatory repatriation could not be enforced. No matter how much I wanted to, I would not be able to get into Sierra Leone. As with other Sierra Leoneans, I was eligible for temporary protected status until the war subsided.

My attorney was busy. She had spoken with New Physicians for Wisconsin on my behalf, and they were eager for well-trained pediatricians to fill the underserved positions both among the Indian tribes in Wisconsin and the inner city clinics that serve the poor. She told the organization, "If you can show that you have exhausted your search for American citizen physicians to fill these positions, you can file for Permanent Residency for Dr. Davies."

They replied, "We have advertised everywhere and have been unable to fill these positions."

After talking to her at length, I completed my application for any pediatric post with New Physicians for Wisconsin. Even before I got the news that I was hired to serve in the inner city clinic in

Milwaukee, I received word from the INS that I had been granted U.S. Permanent Residency status—and my Green Card was in the mail.

High we exalt thee, realm of the free;
Great is the love we have for thee;
. . . Land that we love, our Sierra Leone.

Someone was blaring the words of the Sierra Leone national anthem in my head. I would fall asleep to this song for years to come.

Ironic. Bittersweet.

CHAPTER SEVENTEEN

LIVING THE DREAM

Everything I had crossed the ocean for was becoming a reality, but was this feeling one of misgiving? Ah! It was all happening on the wrong side of the Atlantic!

A disquiet settled in the pit of my stomach. The Sierra Leone national anthem would not leave my head. I complained to anyone who would listen: "I should be taking all this knowledge to my home country. The people there are poor and in desperate need."

In exasperation my attorney finally said, "Glena, there are poor people here too!" So I accepted the position as pediatrician at the Issac Coggs Health Center in Milwaukee.

Being a pediatrician was the easy part. Soon I was dealing not only with the health needs of infants and children, but the tangled webs of family life in an area that was known for drugs, crime, and fatherless households.

At times I felt like a social worker, making house calls to follow up on patients I was extremely concerned about. In many cases, I had to interact with the police when children were caught in the crosshairs of crime and negligence. The negligence was often rampant throughout the entire system.

One evening, in an outrage, I drove a twelve-year-old girl who had been repeatedly raped by her mother's boyfriend to the police station. Social Services had labeled her a runaway, and no one had bothered to examine her.

I admitted her to the hospital and made notes in her chart of my findings. To my horror, she was discharged the next day on the recommendation of Social Services.

Fortunately the girl skipped school and returned to find me. I was about to put her in my car and head for the police station when the nursing director of our clinic tried to stop me. "You don't know if this is a setup," she said. "This girl may have a gun."

I threw the child's backpack in my trunk and drove her to the police station and was paralyzed by the officer's response. "You must be new around here. We see this all the time."

He took my report and made note of my demand that the mother's boyfriend be prosecuted. I found out later that the girl was simply returned to her mother's home.

Not all the cases were heartbreaking. I urgently referred a thirteen-year-old boy for exploratory surgery when I found his right scrotal sac empty, with no testicle. He had not been seen by a doctor since he was discharged at birth. During the surgery, they found nonviable testicular fragments that would have increased his risk for testicular cancer.

After surgery the young man was most impressed with the prosthetic testicle which had been implanted in the empty right sac to make him look more esthetically balanced.

We were both happy, but for different reasons.

Post surgery, whenever he came to our clinic, he would hug me and whisper, "I'm hanging real good," and we would both chuckle.

My years at Isaac Coggs were filled with experiences too numerous to detail here. My time there opened many doors that allowed me to teach medical students and residents of the Medical College of Wisconsin, where I had admitting privileges at the Children's Hospital of Wisconsin. This exposure later led to interaction with other community physicians who invited me to join Falls Medical Group, a private practice group in southeast Wisconsin. I remained a partner and practiced there for two decades, serving over five thousand patients.

Citizen Sisi

Sisi came with Sean and me to Wisconsin. Although at first she had a difficult time adjusting to the culture, friends at First Baptist continually reached out to her. Slowly, she started enjoying some independence.

Sisi was resentful that she hadn't had as much schooling as her brothers, but at the age of eighty, she became a U.S. citizen. She amazed everyone by not only memorizing all the amendments to the U.S. Constitution, but also learning the names of all the members of the House of Representatives and all the Senators. She would later chastise anyone who visited her and did not know who their senator was. This was a woman who, given just a fraction of the education her children received, would have become a force to contend with. A proud, secure woman emerged at her swearing in ceremony, where she was saluted and presented with the American flag.

She died in 2010 at the age of ninety-two in Virginia, where she had moved to be near Olive and Ian who had both settled there.

Loss

I have come to realize that loss is nothing but change—from the expected to the unexpected. Change, however, does not walk alone. In her youth she clings to despair, yearning, and sorrow.

Sorrow is that unyielding selfish desert that binds and immobilizes you. Her chill clings like the morning dew; the soul becomes quiet.

In the still of the night, I hear the voice in my head say, "But for my indiscretion with John, even motherhood would have been, to me, a membership of exclusion."

I think of the homeland that does not recognize me as her own, and I am awash with sorrow. It is in these moments of sadness that the old movie plot plays again—the one where I see in my mind's eye my ancestors on the beaches of Sierra Leone, facing west, bound in chains . . . with no hope, no name. Just waves crashing on the shores, marking time.

In my reverie, three generations have passed; these ancestors are now on the beaches of Nova Scotia, facing east . . . bound by poverty, yoked with the names of their previous masters as their only possession.

The waves of the Atlantic continue to crash, undeterred. Now it's my turn. The mist of the waves sprays across my face. I am standing on the beach, facing west, fettered by poverty, clinging to the promise of things imagined. The Atlantic Ocean will take me to a place that promises abundance, where the tired and hungry are sought and welcomed. I huddle with the masses; no chains bind me, save the burning, unrelenting desire to stand apart. My diplomas are the tripod I use to stand and steady myself with each passing wave of crisis.

New laws, unfair laws, force me back into the water once more. I trudge eastbound toward that now-familiar ocean, the Atlantic, undeterred, girded with grit. In time I learn to be cradled and comforted by the gentle sound of its ebb and flow.

Then suddenly, shots ring out in the distance, jarring me out of any coziness I may have nestled into. Closer and closer come the perilous bullets.

The now turbulent waves engulf and carry me westward. *Give me your tired, your poor, your huddled masses.* I try to recall the words. *Yearning to break free.* Yearning to eat, sleep, and hope. *Give me these, the wretched refuse of your teeming shores. Send these, homeless, dispossessed of the lands they cry out for, but run from. Send these. Then hope and pray that the fog of shame, degradation, doubt, and fear that shrouds them will lift.*

I am tired.

Finally I see the torch and the tablet-bearing lady—and at her feet the broken chains.

Is this where *my* chains will be broken? I can only hope.

The dream never dies.

With age, change partners with learning, strength, and resilience. It is then that we learn to see that nothing really is ever lost.

CHAPTER EIGHTEEN
FULL CIRCLE

I am now retired, living in the township of Fort Mill, South Carolina, in the subdivision of Eppington South. Until I bought a plane ticket to go there, I had never heard of Fort Mill.

I am convinced that this was no accident. My bus has all four of its wheels turning. My Driver and I are parked here in Fort Mill, perhaps to help me fill in the missing portions of my knowledge of the part South Carolina played in the lives of those ancestors who journeyed westward, bound in chains. The minute I arrived in Fort Mill, I could see and smell the jessamine bushes all around me. This is the state flower of South Carolina.

As soon as I repeated the word *jessamine*, I no longer heard my own voice. Instead, I heard that old familiar voice of Grandma Constance as we brushed past that "jessamine" bush in the compound in Bonthe.

The jessamine bushes seem to beckon; they almost seem to be saying, "Come. Tarry here with me a while." South Carolina is a state from which some slaves fled to Nova Scotia and then on to Freetown, Sierra Leone.

Fort Mill is full of history. A three-mile drive from my house takes me to Confederate Park, established in 1891, which holds the monument to white men who defended South Carolina against the "northern aggression." In school I was taught it was called the Civil War.

I often wondered why the "Kill Me Quick" vans in Sierra Leone often displayed Latin phrases on their windshields. A very common one was *Dum Spiro Spero*, which means "While I Breathe, I Hope."

I would chuckle each time I imagined what they were hoping for—extra wheels, extra struts? One could easily make homogenized milk by just riding in any of these bone-shaking vans!

It wasn't until I closely examined the monument at Confederate Park that I saw where the Sons of the Confederacy displayed their motto. *Dum Spiro Spero* it reads on the flag.

As with names, the slaves took those words of their masters. What else did they have? They remembered the names of the flowers whose fragrance must have comforted them. Now they had *Dum Spiro Spero*—they had hope, which they carried with them, and which their children's children now carry.

Within five miles, at the Old Colored Presbyterian Cemetery, I can see and touch the gravestone of Lucy Phifer. It reads, "Born a slave in 1844—Died January 3, 1930." I hold in my hand a copy of a manifest that shows Lucy and her husband, Jack, both now free, traveling from Fort Mill via Brooklyn, New York, to Freetown, Sierra Leone, en route to Liberia. The story of her crossing seems eerily familiar. She made safe passage, but despite her best efforts, the challenges she faced forced her to ride the tumultuous swells of the Atlantic westward. She had lost several children, but on her return she was accompanied by her daughter Lillee (Lily)—who survived but lost a leg from an infected insect bite.

Lucy returned to Fort Mill where she resumed work as a domestic in the household of Esther Phifer Allison, relative of Lucy's former slave master, George Caleb Phifer.

When I found a photograph of Lillee Jane Phifffer in attendance at the Anne Springs Close wedding, I had to go and see Mrs. Close. Anne Springs is herself a living legend of Fort Mill. She was gracious; it was like looking into the face of history.

When I moved here, my address of Eppington South Drive had very little meaning until I spent hours at the local history museum. Walking the two-and-a-half miles of my neighborhood, the names of the streets and lanes jump to life. The subdivision is named for many of the Epps family who have lived in this immediate area for approximately five generations. The names of the Epps who were "Defenders of State Sovereignty" are etched in the two monuments erected at Confederate Park—and those of their descendants adorn most of the streets of the Eppington South neighborhood.

A recently rediscovered potter's field near a neighbor's home brought me great excitement. The last burial purportedly occurred there in 1895 and was witnessed by my neighbor, Roy Epp's aunt.

Often I go to sit there among the unmarked stones and wonder who these people were. Had slaves been buried there? If so, are any of my ancestors among them?

I garden avidly, but I also spend time piecing together any information I can glean about my legacy. Even as I search, I fully expect to find that the land to which my Palmer, Roberts, Davies, and Thompson ancestors were repatriated may not have been the land from which they were taken. My autosomal DNA shows 97.4 percent African and 2.6 percent European ancestry. We can infer that the intimate contact documented historically between slaves and their owners did occur in my family. While we tarry here, further DNA testing may well help the next generation put together the pieces of who they are and where they are from.

Making a Difference

Retirement has afforded me much time for reflection. Whenever I worry about whether I did enough to make a difference, one of my most challenging patients comes to mind. By age seventeen he had joined a gang, suffered two concussions, had a severe eye injury, broke several fingers during fist fights, was truant most of the school year, and abused drugs. He often cursed at my nurses or other staff.

At my retirement party, I was surprised to see him. He brought me a letter expressing regret for his past behavior. "So now that I've cleaned up my act, you decide to leave me?" he asked. "Why?"

"Because now you know the way," I told him. I was moved to tears.

This was the child that, in desperation, motivated me to call an after-hours meeting, inviting his teachers, parents, grandparents, siblings, and anyone else who cared to come. I told them that although I had a prescription pad to write a script for antibiotics, what ailed this boy was not treatable with medication. I let them know that he was at risk of dying young, and I challenged them with my well-used phrase, "If the elders do not stand up for him, the idiots will!"

I admonished them to treat him like a community project. Even his enabling grandmother, who provided him with financial resources, pitched in to help. To see him at my farewell celebration gave me great satisfaction.

The years roll by and changes take place, bringing opportunities to sing a new song.

Welcome to Parenthood

My son, Sean, never got to see Africa or know the Africa I know. He is married now, and he and his wife, Whitney, have two sons, Abram and Darren. The day his first son was born, I wrote him this letter:

Dear Sean:
WELCOME TO PARENTHOOD—that society into which one must be invited, which cannot be bought, assigned or inherited.

Today, your name is now entered into the genetic book of immortality, and so your genes will begin to dance on the world stage. Starting now, you will develop Darwinian eyes as you watch your genes in full display.

As you well know, I have cornered the "Worry Market." I worry about everything. Thankfully, I am NOT at all worried about you becoming a parent. I am joyful. Nay, ecstatic!

I worried that I would never be invited to parenthood when I saw my chance at parenthood melt away with my husband's infidelity, but happily things didn't go that way, and here we are.

Little did I know how much you were going to teach me. So now I will share a few tips about parenting (as you know I never pass up on a chance to teach):

This will be a time, a passage really, through which you will discover yourself in the world. It will be fraught with challenges and joys far surpassing any wild ride you may have enjoyed at a fair. You may discover what true sacrifice means. For me, I watched my own mother give up her meals so that her children could eat. You may come to understand selflessness when you are called upon to give up on a dream so that your child or children can succeed.

Like my mother before me, we don't let things happen to us. We make things happen to us. We don't allow people to call us just anything. We decide what we answer to.

In that light, I must tell you WHO YOU ARE FROM—who some of the dancers were:

Great-Grandma Constance—a woman so full of compassion for others that I instantly recognized a similar spirit when I met Joanne Gygax. Fortunately, you were a beneficiary of Joanne's love and affection, and so I believe that you somehow met Grandma Constance.

Grandma May—the Tiger, the grit, the no-nonsense "get it done now, at all cost, or die trying" kind of soul, whose soul was tried mercilessly and who herself sometimes forgot to show mercy.

Grandfather Joshua Okoro—the bright, carefree, adaptable, thinks outside the box, not drawn to Pomp and Circumstance, who often appeared crude and crass.

Father John J.—very often you can hear him say, "Those who love me call me Johnny," whose wit and easy charm is so evident in your smile and grace but whose cowardice has left so many broken.

Mother Glena—your enigma. The one who hears your drumbeats in her head and tries to understand its cadence but not change it. The process often can be described as "The Clash of the Titans." Hahahaha!

THIS IS YOUR INHERITANCE!
This is a time of new beginnings, during which you may be dismayed,

encouraged, proud, sad, and anxious as you watch with your new Darwinian eyes. Sometimes you may see some of these old characters dancing in new bodies.

My father and your father both denied themselves this wonderment with the choices they made.

You and I both feel a keen sense of loss by their absence. I would like to challenge you to believe that loss has molded us. Loss changes people.

So before I relinquish my position as teacher and begin to revel in your journey as you mentor your children, a few admonitions:

DO NOT DO EASY THINGS
It is easy to love pretty things, nice things,
good-looking people, rich people.
It is equally easy
to harm ugly things, gross things,
to dismiss those different from you,
to mistreat those weaker than you
to marginalize those less skilled than you.
So don't do easy things—abandon harshness.

I close now with a prayer that I'm paraphrasing from a book I recently read.

> "It is with humble gratitude, O God, that we seek blessings on Abram, Whitney, Sean, and the countless ancestors who have bequeathed to them a rich heritage with which they are blessed. We give thanks for their sacrifices and vision. As our histories and values become woven into life's tapestries of the

next generation, keep us mindful of our many and bountiful blessings, and of our love for and responsibilities to one another. AMEN.